CONNECTED MATHEMATICS® 3

Statistics and Data Analysis

Glenda Lappan, Elizabeth Difanis Phillips,
James T. Fey, Susan N. Friel

PEARSON

Boston, Massachusetts • Chandler, Arizona • Glenview, Illinois • Hoboken, New Jersey

Connected Mathematics® was developed at Michigan State University with financial support from the Michigan State University Office of the Provost, Computing and Technology, and the College of Natural Science.

This material is based upon work supported by the National Science Foundation under Grant No. MDR 9150217 and Grant No. ESI 9986372. Opinions expressed are those of the authors and not necessarily those of the Foundation.

As with prior editions of this work, the authors and administration of Michigan State University preserve a tradition of devoting royalties from this publication to support activities sponsored by the MSU Mathematics Education Enrichment Fund.

Acknowledgments appear on page 132, which constitutes an extension of this copyright page.

13-digit ISBN 978-0-13-327637-4
10-digit ISBN 0-13-327637-6
6 7 8 9 10 V011 17 16 15

PEARSON

A Team of Experts

Glenda Lappan is a University Distinguished Professor in the Program in Mathematics Education (PRIME) and the Department of Mathematics at Michigan State University. Her research and development interests are in the connected areas of students' learning of mathematics and mathematics teachers' professional growth and change related to the development and enactment of K–12 curriculum materials.

Elizabeth Difanis Phillips is a Senior Academic Specialist in the Program in Mathematics Education (PRIME) and the Department of Mathematics at Michigan State University. She is interested in teaching and learning mathematics for both teachers and students. These interests have led to curriculum and professional development projects at the middle school and high school levels, as well as projects related to the teaching and learning of algebra across the grades.

James T. Fey is a Professor Emeritus at the University of Maryland. His consistent professional interest has been development and research focused on curriculum materials that engage middle and high school students in problem-based collaborative investigations of mathematical ideas and their applications.

Susan N. Friel is a Professor of Mathematics Education in the School of Education at the University of North Carolina at Chapel Hill. Her research interests focus on statistics education for middle-grade students and, more broadly, on teachers' professional development and growth in teaching mathematics K–8.

With... Yvonne Grant and Jacqueline Stewart

Yvonne Grant teaches mathematics at Portland Middle School in Portland, Michigan. Jacqueline Stewart is a recently retired high school teacher of mathematics at Okemos High School in Okemos, Michigan. Both Yvonne and Jacqueline have worked on a variety of activities related to the development, implementation, and professional development of the CMP curriculum since its beginning in 1991.

Development Team

CMP3 Authors

Glenda Lappan, University Distinguished Professor, Michigan State University
Elizabeth Difanis Phillips, Senior Academic Specialist, Michigan State University
James T. Fey, Professor Emeritus, University of Maryland
Susan N. Friel, Professor, University of North Carolina – Chapel Hill

With...

Yvonne Grant, Portland Middle School, Michigan
Jacqueline Stewart, Mathematics Consultant, Mason, Michigan

In Memory of... William M. Fitzgerald, Professor (Deceased), Michigan State University, who made substantial contributions to conceptualizing and creating CMP1.

Administrative Assistant

Michigan State University
Judith Martus Miller

Support Staff

Michigan State University
Undergraduate Assistants:
Bradley Robert Corlett, Carly Fleming, Erin Lucian, Scooter Nowak

Development Assistants

Michigan State University
Graduate Research Assistants:
Richard "Abe" Edwards, Nic Gilbertson, Funda Gonulates, Aladar Horvath, Eun Mi Kim, Kevin Lawrence, Jennifer Nimtz, Joanne Philhower, Sasha Wang

Assessment Team

Maine
Falmouth Public Schools
Falmouth Middle School: Shawn Towle

Michigan
Ann Arbor Public Schools
Tappan Middle School
Anne Marie Nicoll-Turner

Portland Public Schools
Portland Middle School
Holly DeRosia, Yvonne Grant

Traverse City Area Public Schools
Traverse City East Middle School
Jane Porath, Mary Beth Schmitt

Traverse City West Middle School
Jennifer Rundio, Karrie Tufts

Ohio
Clark-Shawnee Local Schools
Rockway Middle School: Jim Mamer

Content Consultants

Michigan State University
Peter Lappan, Professor Emeritus, Department of Mathematics

Normandale Community College
Christopher Danielson, Instructor, Department of Mathematics & Statistics

University of North Carolina – Wilmington
Dargan Frierson, Jr., Professor, Department of Mathematics & Statistics

Student Activities

Michigan State University
Brin Keller, Associate Professor, Department of Mathematics

Consultants

Indiana
Purdue University
Mary Bouck, Mathematics Consultant

Michigan
Oakland Schools
Valerie Mills, Mathematics Education
Supervisor
Mathematics Education Consultants:
Geraldine Devine, Dana Gosen

Ellen Bacon, Independent Mathematics
Consultant

New York
University of Rochester
Jeffrey Choppin, Associate Professor

Ohio
University of Toledo
Debra Johanning, Associate Professor

Pennsylvania
University of Pittsburgh
Margaret Smith, Professor

Texas
University of Texas at Austin
Emma Trevino, Supervisor of
Mathematics Programs, The Dana Center

Mathematics for All Consulting
Carmen Whitman, Mathematics Consultant

....

Reviewers

Michigan
Ionia Public Schools
Kathy Dole, Director of Curriculum
and Instruction

Grand Valley State University
Lisa Kasmer, Assistant Professor

Portland Public Schools
Teri Keusch, Classroom Teacher

Minnesota
Hopkins School District 270
Michele Luke, Mathematics Coordinator

....

Field Test Sites for CMP3

Michigan
Ann Arbor Public Schools
Tappan Middle School
Anne Marie Nicoll-Turner*

Portland Public Schools
Portland Middle School: Mark Braun,
Angela Buckland, Holly DeRosia,
Holly Feldpausch, Angela Foote,
Yvonne Grant*, Kristin Roberts,
Angie Stump, Tammi Wardwell

Traverse City Area Public Schools
Traverse City East Middle School
Ivanka Baic Berkshire, Brenda Dunscombe,
Tracie Herzberg, Deb Larimer, Jan Palkowski,
Rebecca Perreault, Jane Porath*,
Robert Sagan, Mary Beth Schmitt*

Traverse City West Middle School
Pamela Alfieri, Jennifer Rundio,
Maria Taplin, Karrie Tufts*

Maine
Falmouth Public Schools
Falmouth Middle School: Sally Bennett,
Chris Driscoll, Sara Jones, Shawn Towle*

Minnesota
Minneapolis Public Schools
Jefferson Community School
Leif Carlson*,
Katrina Hayek Munsisoumang*

Ohio
Clark-Shawnee Local Schools
Reid School: Joanne Gilley
Rockway Middle School: Jim Mamer*
Possum School: Tami Thomas

*Indicates a Field Test Site Coordinator

Data About Us

Statistics and Data Analysis

1 What's in a Name? Organizing, Representing, and Describing Data 8

2 Who's in Your Household? Using the Mean 34

3

What's Your Favorite...? Measuring Variability   58

4

What Numbers Describe Us? Using Graphs to Group Data   85

Looking Ahead

What is the greatest number of pets owned by the students in your class? How can you find out?

How much do the sugar contents of different kinds of cereals vary?

How can you determine which of two basketball teams has taller players? Older players?

Charlestown Spartans

Player	Age	Height (cm)
#37	23	185
#29	27	173
#56	19	204
#39	35	202
#28	32	190
#16	33	209
#25	30	189

Part of a biologist's job is to collect data on organisms, such as coral. They do this to understand the organism and its role in the world. Not all coral is the same, so biologists study many corals in order to learn more about the species as a whole.

In a similar way, the United States government gathers information about its citizens. They do this to learn more about the population as a whole. Collecting data from every household in the United States is a huge task. So, many surveys involve gathering information from much smaller groups of people.

People often make statements about the results of surveys. It is important to understand these statements. For example, what does it mean when reports say that the average middle-school student watches three hours of television on a weekday and has four people in his or her family?

In *Data About Us*, you will learn to collect and analyze data. You will also learn to use your results to describe people and their characteristics.

Mathematical Highlights

Data About Us

In *Data About Us,* you will learn different ways to collect, organize, display, and analyze data.

In this Unit you will learn to:

- Use the process of data investigation by posing questions, collecting and analyzing data, and interpreting the data to answer questions

- Organize and represent data using tables, dot plots, line plots, bar graphs, histograms, and box-and-whisker plots

- Describe the overall shape of a distribution and identify whether or not it is symmetrical around a central value

- Compute the mean, median, and mode of a data distribution, and use these measures to indicate what is typical for the distribution

- Describe the variability of a distribution by identifying clusters and gaps, and by calculating the range, Interquartile Range (IQR), and Mean Absolute Deviation (MAD)

- Identify which statistical measures of center and spread should be used to describe a particular distribution of data

- Distinguish between categorical data and numerical data, and identify which graphs and statistics may be used to represent each type of data

- Compare two or more distributions of data, including using measures of center and spread to make comparisons

When you encounter a new problem, it is a good idea to ask yourself questions. In this Unit, you might ask questions such as:

What question is being investigated to collect these data?

How might I organize the data?

What statistical measures will help describe the distribution of data?

What will these statistical measures tell me about the distribution of the data?

How can I use graphs and statistics to report an answer to my original question?

Mathematical Practices and Habits of Mind

In the *Connected Mathematics* curriculum you will develop an understanding of important mathematical ideas by solving problems and reflecting on the mathematics involved. Every day, you will use "habits of mind" to make sense of problems and apply what you learn to new situations. Some of these habits are described by the *Common Core State Standards for Mathematical Practices* (MP).

MP1 Make sense of problems and persevere in solving them.

When using mathematics to solve a problem, it helps to think carefully about

- data and other facts you are given and what additional information you need to solve the problem;
- strategies you have used to solve similar problems and whether you could solve a related simpler problem first;
- how you could express the problem with equations, diagrams, or graphs;
- whether your answer makes sense.

MP2 Reason abstractly and quantitatively.

When you are asked to solve a problem, it often helps to

- focus first on the key mathematical ideas;
- check that your answer makes sense in the problem setting;
- use what you know about the problem setting to guide your mathematical reasoning.

MP3 Construct viable arguments and critique the reasoning of others.

When you are asked to explain why a conjecture is correct, you can

- show some examples that fit the claim and explain why they fit;
- show how a new result follows logically from known facts and principles.

When you believe a mathematical claim is incorrect, you can

- show one or more counterexamples—cases that don't fit the claim;
- find steps in the argument that do not follow logically from prior claims.

MP4 Model with mathematics.

When you are asked to solve problems, it often helps to

- think carefully about the numbers or geometric shapes that are the most important factors in the problem, then ask yourself how those factors are related to each other;
- express data and relationships in the problem with tables, graphs, diagrams, or equations, and check your result to see if it makes sense.

MP5 Use appropriate tools strategically.

When working on mathematical questions, you should always

- decide which tools are most helpful for solving the problem and why;
- try a different tool when you get stuck.

MP6 Attend to precision.

In every mathematical exploration or problem-solving task, it is important to

- think carefully about the required accuracy of results; is a number estimate or geometric sketch good enough, or is a precise value or drawing needed?
- report your discoveries with clear and correct mathematical language that can be understood by those to whom you are speaking or writing.

MP7 Look for and make use of structure.

In mathematical explorations and problem solving, it is often helpful to

- look for patterns that show how data points, numbers, or geometric shapes are related to each other;
- use patterns to make predictions.

MP8 Look for and express regularity in repeated reasoning.

When results of a repeated calculation show a pattern, it helps to

- express that pattern as a general rule that can be used in similar cases;
- look for shortcuts that will make the calculation simpler in other cases.

You will use all of the Mathematical Practices in this Unit. Sometimes, when you look at a Problem, it is obvious which practice is most helpful. At other times, you will decide on a practice to use during class explorations and discussions. After completing each Problem, ask yourself:

- What mathematics have I learned by solving this Problem?
- What Mathematical Practices were helpful in learning this mathematics?

Unit Project

Is Anyone Typical?

What are the characteristics of a typical middle-school student? Does a typical middle-school student really exist? As you proceed through this Unit, you will identify some "typical" facts about your classmates, such as:

- The typical number of letters in a student's full name
- The typical number of people in a student's household
- The typical height of a student

After you have completed the Investigations in *Data About Us,* you will carry out a statistical investigation to answer the question,

"What are some of the characteristics of a typical middle-school student?"

These characteristics may include:

- Physical characteristics (such as age, height, or eye color)
- Family and home characteristics (such as number of siblings or number of computers)
- Behaviors (such as hobbies or number of hours spent watching television)
- Preferences, opinions, or attitudes (such as favorite musical group or choice for class president)

As you work through this Unit, make and refine your plans for your project. Keep in mind that a statistical investigation involves posing questions, collecting data, analyzing data, and interpreting the results of the analysis. As you work through each Investigation, think about how you might use what you are learning to complete your project.

What's in a Name? Organizing, Representing, and Describing Data

People are naturally curious about themselves and others. As you work on this Unit, make notes on how you would describe the "typical" middle-school student. At the end of the Unit, you will use what you have learned to conduct a statistical investigation.

Statistical problem solving involves using data to answer questions. The Problems in each Investigation will help you to think about the steps in a statistical investigation. This involves

- asking a question,

- collecting data,

- analyzing the data,

- interpreting the results and writing a report to answer the question asked.

You have already used bar graphs, line plots, and tables to organize and compare data. In *Data About Us,* you will use other tools and representations.

....

Common Core State Standards

6.SP.A.2 Understand that a set of data collected to answer a statistical question has a distribution that can be described by its center, spread, and overall shape.

6.SP.B.4 Display numerical data in plots on a number line, including dot plots...

6.SP.B.5a Summarize numerical data sets in relation to their context, such as by reporting the number of observations.

Also 6.SP.A.1, 6.SP.A.3, 6.SP.B.5c

1.1 How Many Letters Are in a Name?

Names are filled with tradition. *Onomatologists* study names to discover clues about family ancestors or where people settled around the world. One characteristic that you might not think about is the *length* of a person's name.

There are times when name length matters. Computers may truncate, or shorten, a long name on a library card or an e-mail address. Likewise, only a limited number of letters may fit on a friendship bracelet.

In Problem 1.1, a middle-school class is studying various countries in Asia, as shown in the map below. The class is pen pals with a class in China.

The table on the next page shows the names of the 30 students in each class. Next to the names are the **data** values or *observations* for name length—the total number of letters in the first and last names of each student.

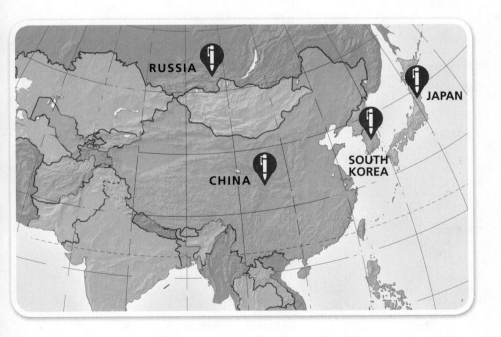

Name Lengths Table 1

Chinese Students	Number of Letters	U.S. Students	Number of Letters
Hua Gao	6	Carson Alexander	15
Liu Gao	6	Avery Anderson	13
Xiang Guo	8	Makayla Bell	11
Zhang Guo	8	Hunter Bennett	13
Li Han	5	Jacob Campbell	13
Yu Han	5	Alexandria Clark	15
Miao He	6	Antonio Cook	11
Yu Hu	4	Kaitlyn Cooper	13
Kong Huang	9	Takisha Davis	12
Ping Li	6	Rebecca Diaz	11
Li Liang	7	Sofia Garcia	11
Chen Lin	7	Arlo Gonzales	12
Yanlin Liu	9	Elijah Hall	10
Dan Luo	6	Kaori Hashimoto	14
Lin Ma	5	Dalton Hayes	11
Lin Song	7	Noah Henderson	13
Chi Sun	6	Haley Jenkins	12
Bai Tang	7	Jack Kelly	9
Dewei Wang	9	Bryce Moore	10
Zhou Wu	6	Lillian Richardson	17
Yun Xiao	7	Liam Rogers	10
Hua Xie	6	Savannah Russell	15
Le Xu	4	Kyle Simmons	11
Xiang Xu	7	Adam Smith	9
Chi Yang	7	Marissa Thomas	13
Qiao Zhang	9	Danielle Thompson	16
Zheng Zhao	9	Esperanza Torres	15
Yang Zheng	9	Ethan Ward	9
Chung Zhou	9	Mackenzie Wilson	15
Wu Zhu	5	Nathaniel Young	14

- An **attribute** is a characteristic or feature about a person or object. What attribute is being investigated here?

- How are the data values for the 60 observations determined?

- What graphs might you make to organize and compare this information?

- Compare the name lengths of the U.S. students to the name lengths of the Chinese students. What do you notice?

In this Problem, you will represent data with tables and graphs in order to examine their **distribution**—the shape of the data set as a whole.

Problem 1.1

A A **frequency table** shows the number of times each value in a data set occurs. It arranges observations in order from least to greatest with their corresponding frequencies.

The frequency table shows some of the data about the Chinese class. The lengths of the first seven names (Hua Gao through Miao He) are recorded using tally marks.

Lengths of Chinese Names (From Name Lengths Table 1)		
Number of Letters	Tally	Frequency
1		0
2		0
3		0
4		■
5	||	■
6	|||	■
7		■
8	||	■
9		■

continued on the next page >

Problem 1.1 *continued*

1. **a.** Some name lengths do not occur, such as a name one letter long. How does the table show this?

   b. On a copy of the table, complete the entries for the Chinese class.

2. For the U.S. class data, make a frequency table like the one on the previous page.

3. Compare the two frequency tables of class data.

   a. What are the shortest and longest Chinese names?

   b. What are the shortest and longest U.S. names?

B A **line plot** is a graph that shows data values on a number line using **X**s or other marks.

1. Make two line plots, one for each class. Use the same *scale* on both line plots.

2. Describe how the frequency tables helped you make the line plots.

C Use the line plots you made in Question B. Look at the shapes of the distributions of the data sets.

1. How would you describe the *shape* of the distribution? Are there any places where the data values **cluster,** or group together? Are there any **gaps,** or places where there are no data values?

2. Write two questions about the Chinese and U.S. classes that you can answer from your graphs.

3. Write three statements to compare the name lengths of the U.S. students and the Chinese students.

4. Describe how the line plots helped you compare the name lengths for the two classes.

D 1. Identify a typical name length or name lengths for the Chinese class. Explain your reasoning.

2. Identify a typical name length or name lengths for the U.S. class. Explain your reasoning.

A C E Homework starts on page 19.

1.2 Describing Name Lengths
What Are the Shape, Mode, and Range?

Problem 1.1 asked you to describe a typical name length or name lengths for the U.S. class and for the Chinese class. One way to describe what is *typical* is to identify the data value that occurs most frequently. This is the **mode** of the data set. A data set may have more than one mode. Look back at the graphs you made in Problem 1.1.

• What is the mode of the U.S. class data? The Chinese class data?

In any data set, data values vary from a **minimum value** to a **maximum value.** The difference of the maximum data value and the minimum data value is the **range** of the data.

• What is the range of the U.S. class data? The Chinese class data?

Did You Know?

There are almost 7,000 spoken languages in the world today. Languages change as people of different cultures interact with each other. Some languages have identical or similar alphabets, such as English and Spanish. Other languages, such as Arabic and Japanese, use systems of characters that look quite different from the alphabet that we use in the United States.

The U.S. middle-school class now receives a 20-name list of pen pals from a class in Japan.

Name Lengths Table 2

Japanese Students	Number of Letters
Ai Kiyomizu	10
Daiki Kobayashi	14
Tsubasa Tanaka	13
Eric Katou	9
Kana Hayashi	11
Miyuu Shimizu	12
Ken Satou	8
Manami Ikeda	11
Hina Mori	8
Ryo Takahashi	12
Taka Yamamoto	12
Takumi Itou	10
Haruto Nakamura	14
Tomo Sasaki	10
Youta Kichida	12
Yuki Ine	7
Kiro Suzuki	10
Yumi Matsumoto	13
Yumi Yamasaki	12
Yusuke Yoshida	13

 How do the Japanese name lengths compare to the U.S. name lengths?

In this Problem, you will use *dot plots* to represent the frequency of data. **Dot plots** and line plots are the same types of graphs. Instead of ✗s, dot plots use filled-in circles, or dots.

Problem 1.2

A The students in the U.S. class start making a dot plot to show the distribution of the Japanese name-length data. They record the data values for the first 12 names in the list on the dot plot below.

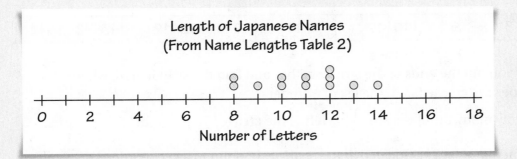

Length of Japanese Names
(From Name Lengths Table 2)

Number of Letters

1. On a copy of the dot plot, insert the data for the last eight names (Haruto Nakamura to Yusuke Yoshida).

2. Look at the shape of the distribution.

   a. Are there *clusters* of data? Explain your reasoning.

   b. Are there gaps in the distribution? Explain.

B 1. What is the *mode* of this distribution?

   2. Is the mode a good description of the typical name length of the Japanese students? Why or why not?

C 1. What is the *range* of the data?

   2. Use the range of each data set to compare the lengths of U.S., Chinese, and Japanese names.

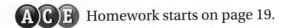 Homework starts on page 19.

1.3 Describing Name Lengths
What Is the Median?

Another way to describe what is typical is to mark the midpoint, or the **median**, of a data set. To identify the median, begin by making an *ordered list* of the data values.

Use a strip of 20 squares from a sheet of grid paper to organize the Japanese pen-pal data from Problem 1.2. Write the name lengths in order from least to greatest on the grid paper, as shown below.

7	8	8	9	10	10	10	10	11	11	12	12	12	12	12	13	13	13	14	14

- If you put the ends of the strip together and fold the strip in half, where does the crease fall in the list of numbers?

- How many numbers are to the left of the crease? To the right?

The median is always located at the "half-way" point in a set of ordered data. Since there are 20 data values, the *position* of the median is at the crease that falls between the 10th and 11th data values. The *value* of the median is determined using the actual values of the 10th and 11th data values.

- What is the median of the data set?

A **summary statistic** is one number calculated from all the data values in a distribution. It summarizes something important about the distribution. The median is a summary statistic. The range and the mode are also summary statistics.

- What can you say about the lengths of the Japanese students' names when you know the median?

Problem 1.3

A The sticky notes below display the name-length data for the Japanese students. The red line shows the *position* of the median, the midpoint of the 20 observations. The *value* of the median is $11\frac{1}{2}$ letters, determined by the 10th and 11th data values of "11" and "12" letters.

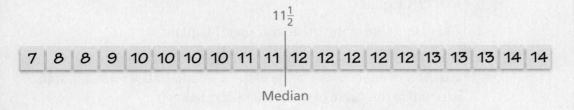

1. The Japanese teacher sent over two more names, Arisa Hasimoto and Yui Inoue. How many observations are there now? What is the *position* of the median? What is the *value* of the median? Explain.

2. One more name, Hina Abe, is added. How many observations are there now? What is the *position* of the median? What is the *value* of the median? Explain.

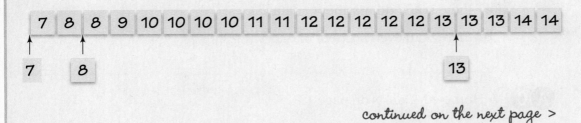

continued on the next page >

Problem 1.3 *continued*

3. The names Aya Yamaguchi, Ayumi Rin, Eri Matsumoto, Haruka Kimura, Kazu Ohayashi, Kazuki Yamada, and Sayake Saitou are added to the list. There are now 30 names from the Japanese class.

   a. Does the position of the median change from its location in part (2)? Explain.

   b. Does the value of the median change? Explain.

   c. Use the complete set of Japanese names. Half of the data values are *less than or equal to* the value of the median. Half are *greater than or equal to* the value of the median. Explain why.

B Compare the Japanese data to the Chinese and U.S. data from Problem 1.1.

1. Identify the value of the median and the range for each of the three data sets.

2. Use these statistics to write at least three statements comparing the three name-length distributions.

C 1. What is the position of the median in a distribution that has 9 data values? 19 data values? 999 data values?

2. What is the position of the median in a distribution that has 10 data values? 20 data values? 1,000 data values?

3. Describe how to locate the position of the median and find the value of the median when

   a. there is an odd number of data values.

   b. there is an even number of data values.

A C E Homework starts on page 19.

Applications

....

For Exercises 1–4, use the table below.

Name Lengths Table 3

Korean Pen Pals	Number of Letters	Korean Pen Pals	Number of Letters
Kim Ae-Cha	8	Hwang Il	7
Lee Chin-Hae	10	Song Ja	6
Park Chin	8	Ahn Jae-Hwa	9
Choi Chung-Cha	12	You Jung	7
Jung Chung-Hee	12	Hong Kang-Dae	11
Kang Bae	7	Kim Hyo-Sonn	10
Cho Dong-Yul	10	Yi Mai-Chin	9
Yoon Eun-Kyung	12	Pak Mi-Ok	7
Chang Hei-Ran	11	Kim Mun-Hee	9
Lim Hak-Kun	9	Yun Myung	8
Han Hei	6	Sin Myung-Hee	11
Shin Hwan	8	Gwon Myung-Ok	11
Suh Eun-Kyung	11	Hong Sang-Ook	11
Kwon Hyun	8	Jeong Shin	9
Son Hyun-Ae	9	Bak Soo	6

1. Make a frequency table and a dot plot for the Korean class data.

2. What are the shortest and longest Korean names?

3. How would you describe the shape of the distribution of Korean data?

4. Identify a typical name length or name lengths for the Korean class data. Explain your reasoning.

5. Recall the name length tables from Problems 1.1 and 1.2 and the names from Exercises 1–4. Below are four dot plots representing each set of names. There are no titles to show which graph represents which set of data.

   a. Write a correct title for each graph, such as *Graph A: Name Lengths From __?__*. Explain your reasoning.

   b. Write four statements that compare the name lengths from the different classes.

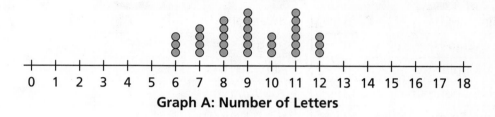

Graph A: Number of Letters

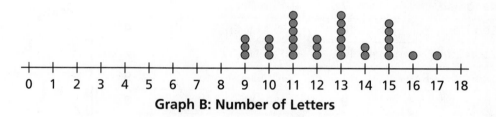

Graph B: Number of Letters

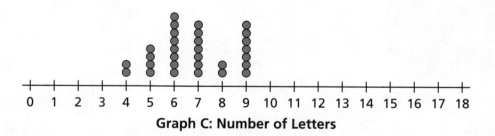

Graph C: Number of Letters

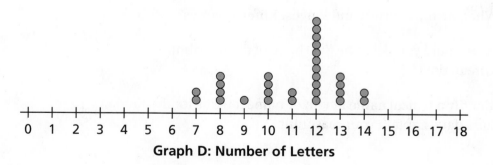

Graph D: Number of Letters

c. Jasmine says that the graphs show a lot of empty space. She thinks the graphs work better if they look like the dot plots below. How are these graphs different from the dot plots displayed in part (b)? Do you agree with Jasmine? Explain your reasoning.

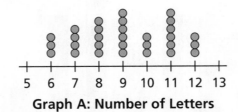

Graph A: Number of Letters

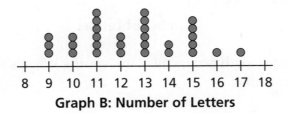

Graph B: Number of Letters

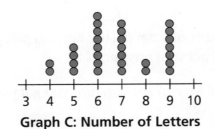

Graph C: Number of Letters

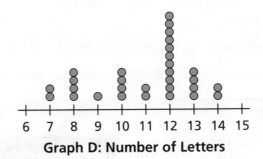

Graph D: Number of Letters

The U.S. class is also pen pals with a Russian class. For Exercises 6–9, use the bar graph below.

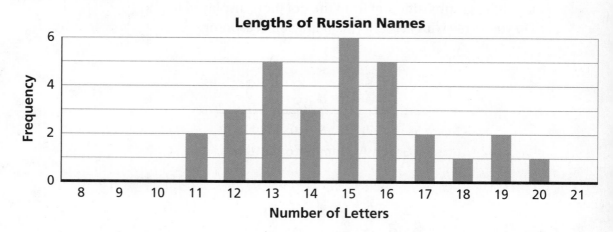

Lengths of Russian Names

6. Which value for name length occurs most frequently? What is this summary statistic called?

7. How many Russian students are in this data set? Explain how you got your answer.

8. What is the range of number of letters in the Russian pen pals' names? Explain how you got your answer.

9. What is the median name length? Explain how you got your answer.

10. Alicia has a pet rat that is 1 year old. She wonders if her rat is old compared to other rats. At the pet store, she finds out that the median lifespan of a rat is 2.5 years.

   a. What does the median tell Alicia about the lifespan of a rat?

   b. What other information would help her predict her rat's lifespan?

Rat Facts

- Rats are gentle and friendly. They bond with their owners and are fun to play with.
- Rats are noctural. They are most active at night.
- Average Lifespan is 2.5 years.
- Rats may be lactose intolerant; be careful in giving them cheese!
- A rat's front teeth could grow up to 5 or 6 inches each year, but they are worn down by gnawing.

Make a line plot for a set of data that fits each description.

11. 24 names that vary in length from 8 letters to 20 letters

12. 7 names with a median length of 14 letters

13. 13 names with a range of 9 letters and a median length of 13 letters

14. 16 names with a median length of $14\frac{1}{2}$ letters and that vary in length from 11 letters to 20 letters

Connections

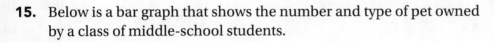

15. Below is a bar graph that shows the number and type of pet owned by a class of middle-school students.

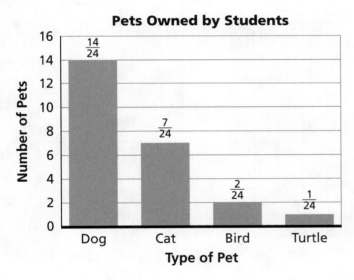

a. The fraction $\frac{14}{24}$ shows the *relative frequency* of pet dogs. What does the numerator tell you? What does the denominator tell you?

b. Can you use the fractions on the bars to determine the number of students surveyed? Explain why or why not.

16. Each grid is numbered 1 to 100. Find the rule that describes the white numbers.

a.

91	92	93	94	95	96	97	98	99	100
81	82	83	84	85	86	87	88	89	90
71	72	73	74	75	76	77	78	79	80
61	62	63	64	65	66	67	68	69	70
51	52	53	54	55	56	57	58	59	60
41	42	43	44	45	46	47	48	49	50
31	32	33	34	35	36	37	38	39	40
21	22	23	24	25	26	27	28	29	30
11	12	13	14	15	16	17	18	19	20
1	2	3	4	5	6	7	8	9	10

b.

91	92	93	94	95	96	97	98	99	100
81	82	83	84	85	86	87	88	89	90
71	72	73	74	75	76	77	78	79	80
61	62	63	64	65	66	67	68	69	70
51	52	53	54	55	56	57	58	59	60
41	42	43	44	45	46	47	48	49	50
31	32	33	34	35	36	37	38	39	40
21	22	23	24	25	26	27	28	29	30
11	12	13	14	15	16	17	18	19	20
1	2	3	4	5	6	7	8	9	10

c.

91	92	93	94	95	96	97	98	99	100
81	82	83	84	85	86	87	88	89	90
71	72	73	74	75	76	77	78	79	80
61	62	63	64	65	66	67	68	69	70
51	52	53	54	55	56	57	58	59	60
41	42	43	44	45	46	47	48	49	50
31	32	33	34	35	36	37	38	39	40
21	22	23	24	25	26	27	28	29	30
11	12	13	14	15	16	17	18	19	20
1	2	3	4	5	6	7	8	9	10

d.

91	92	93	94	95	96	97	98	99	100
81	82	83	84	85	86	87	88	89	90
71	72	73	74	75	76	77	78	79	80
61	62	63	64	65	66	67	68	69	70
51	52	53	54	55	56	57	58	59	60
41	42	43	44	45	46	47	48	49	50
31	32	33	34	35	36	37	38	39	40
21	22	23	24	25	26	27	28	29	30
11	12	13	14	15	16	17	18	19	20
1	2	3	4	5	6	7	8	9	10

17. Make a coordinate grid like the one below. Along the *x*-axis, write the numbers 1 to 30. Do the same for the *y*-axis. For each number on the *x*-axis, plot its factors above it.

The graph below gives part of the answer, showing the factors for numbers 1 through 6.

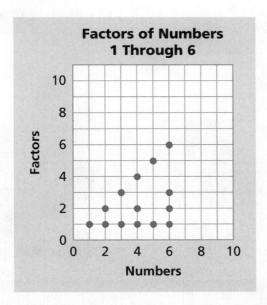

Factors of Numbers 1 Through 6

a. Which numbers have only two factors? What is common about the factors they have?

b. What numbers are even numbers? How can you use their factors to help you answer this question?

c. Make observations about the factors of a number.

i. What is the greatest factor of any number?

ii. What is the least factor of any number?

iii. What is the second-greatest factor of any number? How do these factors relate to the greatest factor of any number?

iv. Make your own observations about the factors of a number.

18. Each graph in parts (a)–(c) is misleading. For each, answer
the following:

- What information is the graph seeking to provide?

- What is wrong with how the information is displayed?

a.
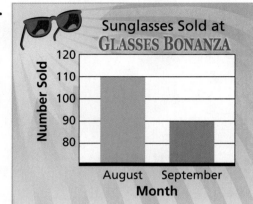

b.
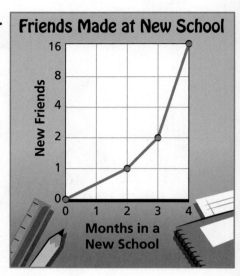

c.

19. The graph below shows the heights of two brothers, Trevor and Trey, over time.

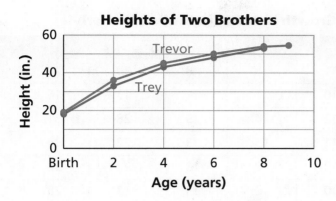

Heights of Two Brothers

a. Write two statements about Trevor's height using the data displayed on the graph.

b. Write two statements about Trey's height using the data displayed on the graph.

c. Write two statements comparing the brothers' heights using the data.

d. Suzanne wrote the statement below. Do you agree with her reasoning? Explain.

> Suzanne:
>
> I know that Trevor is taller than Trey because the line showing his height is above the line showing Trey's height. I also know that Trevor is growing faster than his brother Trey.

20. The table below shows data collected about some gerbil babies and their growth over time.

Growth in Mass (grams) of Six Gerbils

Name	Age in Days					
	11	13	18	20	25	27
Fuzz Ball	10	11	11	13	16	19
Scooter	12	14	19	28	31	36
Sleepy	11	13	13	22	34	38
Racer	12	13	18	22	32	35
Cuddles	10	12	13	17	25	27
Curious	11	12	12	15	19	22

a. Make a graph showing a line for each gerbil's mass on the same coordinate grid. Think carefully about how you label and scale the y-axis (mass) and the x-axis (age in days). Label each line to indicate which gerbil it represents.

b. Write four statements comparing the growth rates of the six gerbils.

c. Suppose someone asks, "About how much do gerbils grow in the first month after they are born?" How would you answer? Explain.

For Exercises 21–23, use the bar graphs below. The graphs show information about a class of middle-school students.

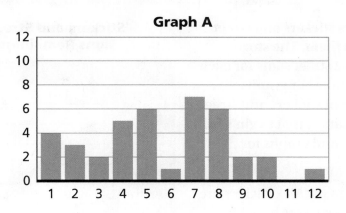

Graph A

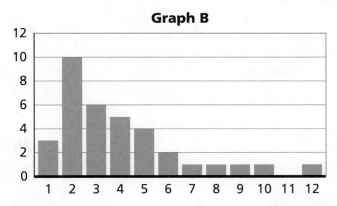

Graph B

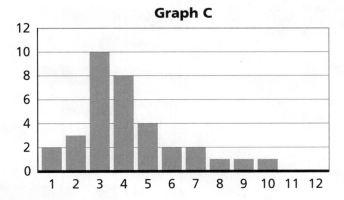

Graph C

21. Which graph might show the number of children in the students' families? Explain.

22. Which graph might show the birth months of the students? Explain.

Note: Months are often written using numbers instead of names. For example, 1 means January, 2 means February, etc.

23. Which graph might show the number of toppings students like on their pizzas? Explain.

Extensions

A greeting card store sells stickers and street signs with first names on them. The store ordered 12 stickers and 12 street signs for each name. The table and the four bar graphs that follow show the numbers of stickers and street signs remaining for the names that begin with the letter A. Use the table and graphs for Exercises 24–30.

24. Use Graph A. How many Alex stickers are left? How many Alex stickers have been sold? Explain.

25. Use Graph B. How many Alex street signs are left? How many Alex street signs have been sold? Explain.

Stickers and Street Signs Remaining

Name	Stickers	Street Signs
Aaron	1	9
Adam	2	7
Alex	7	4
Allison	2	3
Amanda	0	11
Amber	2	3
Amy	3	3
Andrea	2	4
Andrew	8	6
Andy	3	5
Angel	8	4
Ava	10	7

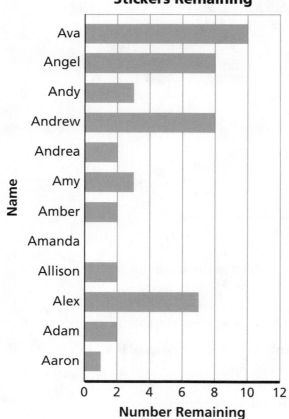

Graph A: Stickers Remaining

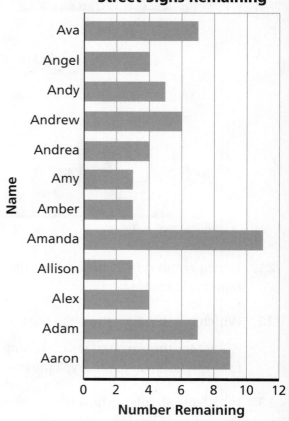

Graph B: Street Signs Remaining

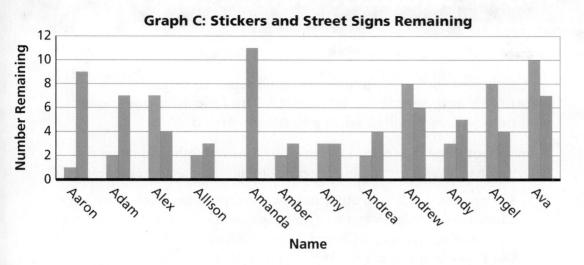

Graph C: Stickers and Street Signs Remaining

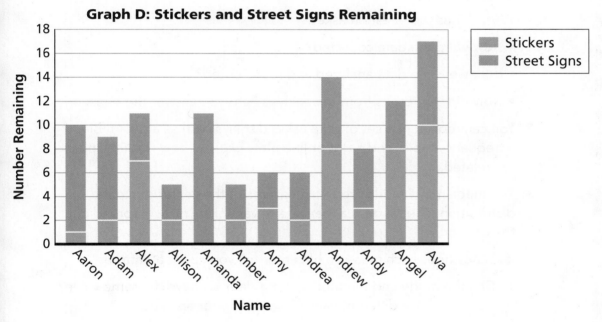

Graph D: Stickers and Street Signs Remaining

26. For names beginning with A, which are more popular, the stickers or the street signs? Explain your answer.

27. If each sticker costs $1.50, how much money has the store collected from selling name stickers that begin with the letter A?

28. For which name has the store sold the most stickers? The least?

29. Graph C is a *double bar graph*. Use this graph to determine the name(s) for which the number of street signs sold and the number of sticker packages sold are the same.

30. Graph D is a *stacked bar graph*. Use this graph to determine whether some names are more popular than others. Justify your answer.

Mathematical Reflections

In this Investigation, you learned some ways to organize, represent, and describe a set of data. The following questions will help you summarize what you have learned.

Think about these questions. Discuss your ideas with other students and your teacher. Then write a summary of your findings in your notebook.

1. The process of carrying out a statistical investigation involves asking a question, gathering and analyzing data, and interpreting the results to answer the question. Choose a data set from this Investigation. Use the data set to answer each question below.

   • **What** was the question asked?

   • **How** were the data collected?

   • **How** were the data analyzed and represented?

   • **How** did the results from the analysis help you answer the question?

2. You can represent a set of data using displays such as a data table, a frequency table, and a dot or line plot. **Explain** how these displays are related.

3. The median and mode are two measures of the center of a data distribution. The range is a measure of variability, or how spread out the data are.

   a. **What** does each measure of center tell you about a data set?

   b. Can the mode and the median for a data set have the same value? Can they have different values? **Explain** your answers.

   c. **How** does the range tell you how much the data vary?

   d. Suppose we add a new data value to a set of data. Does this new value affect the mode? The median? The range? **Explain**.

4. **What** strategies can you use to make comparisons among data sets?

Unit Project

Think about the survey you will be developing.

 How might you collect and display the data you gather?

WHAT'S NEXT

Common Core Mathematical Practices

As you worked on the Problems in this Investigation, you used prior knowledge to make sense of them. You also applied Mathematical Practices to solve the Problems. Think back over your work, the ways you thought about the Problems, and how you used Mathematical Practices.

Nick described his thoughts in the following way:

In Problem 1.1, we used tables and dot plots to show the different sets of data about name lengths. We talked about why we would call each of these data sets a "distribution."

Seeing how the data were distributed across the name lengths, and then noticing things like clusters, gaps, and shape in general, gave us an idea about typical name lengths for each group of students.

When we used the graphs, we made sure to have the same scale on each graph. That made it easier to compare the name lengths of the students from the different countries.

Common Core Standards for Mathematical Practice
MP4 Model with mathematics

- What other Mathematical Practices can you identify in Nick's reasoning?
- Describe a Mathematical Practice that you and your classmates used to solve a different Problem in this Investigation.

Who's in Your Household? Using the Mean

The United States Census is carried out every ten years. Among other statistics, the Census provides useful information about household size. The Census uses the term *household* to mean all the people who live in a "housing unit" (such as a house, an apartment, or a mobile home).

When you work with a set of numbers, a single statistic is often calculated to represent the "typical" value to describe the center of a distribution. In Investigation 1, you used median and mode. Another *measure of center* is the **mean.** It is the most commonly used measure of center for numerical data. The mean of a set of data is often called the *average*.

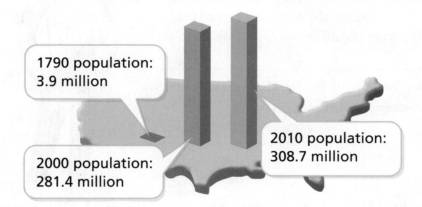

1790 population: 3.9 million

2000 population: 281.4 million

2010 population: 308.7 million

Common Core State Standards

6.SP.A.3 Recognize that a measure of center for a numerical data set summarizes all of its values with a single number . . .

6.SP.B.5b Summarize numerical data sets in relation to their context, such as by describing the nature of the attribute under investigation, including how it was measured and its units of measurement.

6.SP.B.5d Summarize numerical data sets in relation to their context, such as by relating the choice of measures of center . . . to the shape of the data distribution and the context in which the data were gathered.

Also **6.NS.C.6, 6.NS.C.7, 6.SP.A.1, 6.SP.A.2, 6.SP.B.4, 6.SP.B.5a, 6.SP.B.5c**

2.1 What's a Mean Household Size?

Six students in a middle-school class use the United States Census guidelines to find the number of people in their households. Each student made a stack of cubes to show the number of people in his or her household. The stacks show that the six households vary in size.

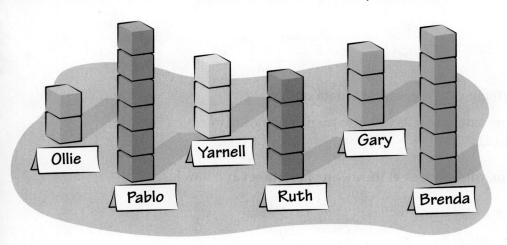

- What is the attribute being investigated?

- How can you use the cube stacks to find the median of the data? The mode?

One way to find the *mean*, or average, household size is to make all the stacks the same height by moving cubes. The evened-out stacks tell you how many people there would be per household if all households were the same size.

- How can you use the cube stacks to find the mean household size for these six students?

You can also use a table to show the data.

Household Size Table 1

Name	Number of People
Ollie	2
Yarnell	3
Gary	3
Ruth	4
Pablo	6
Brenda	6

- How else might you represent this data set?

- Which representation tells you how many people are in all six households?

In this Problem, you will look at the mean of a data set and how it is calculated.

Problem 2.1

A You can use an **ordered-value bar graph** to find the mean of a data set. An ordered-value bar graph and a dot plot are shown below. Both display the number of people in the six households found in Household Size Table 1. You already found the mean, four people, by evening out the cube stacks.

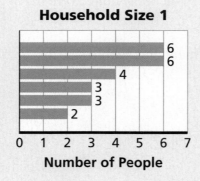

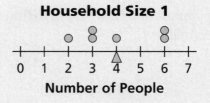

1. Explain how the ordered-value bar graph and dot plot are related.

Problem 2.1 continued

2. Brenda used the ordered-value bar graph at the right to identify the mean. Her first steps are shown. On a copy of the graph, complete Brenda's steps.

3. Ollie says that, after evening out the bars, the graph looks like six households with four people each. How might you have predicted the mean? Explain.

B Another group of students made the table below for a different set of data.

1. Make an ordered-value bar graph and a dot plot to display the data.

2. Find the mean of the data. Explain how you found it.

3. How does the mean of this data set compare to the mean of the data in Question A?

4. How does identifying the mean on an ordered-value bar graph help you find the mean on a dot plot? Explain.

Household Size Table 2

Name	Number of People
Reggie	6
Tara	4
Brendan	3
Felix	4
Hector	3
Tonisha	4

5. Does knowing the mean help you answer the question, "What is the typical household size?" Explain.

A C E Homework starts on page 48.

2.2 Comparing Distributions With the Same Mean

In Problem 2.1, you represented data using dot plots. Another way to represent data is by using a balance.

The picture below shows the frequency of the data from Household Size Table 1. When the fulcrum is located at the mean of the distribution, the ruler is level, as the purple ruler shows. The distribution in Household Size Table 1 balances around 4.

Notice that the green ruler tips to the left. When the fulcrum is not located at the mean of the distribution, the ruler is not level.

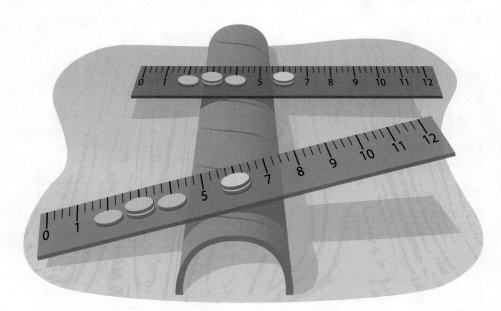

- How does the picture help explain why the mean is often called the *balance point* of a distribution?

- What information do you need to calculate the mean of a data set?

Problem 2.2

A Household Size Table 1 and Household Size Table 2 in Problem 2.1 each show six households with a mean of four people.

   1. Make up a different data set of six households that has a mean of four people per household.

   2. Make an ordered-value bar graph and a line or dot plot to represent your set of data.

   3. Describe how to use your bar graph to verify the mean is four people.

   4. Explain how you can find the following on your graphs:

   a. each person's household size

   b. the total number of households

   c. the total number of people in the combined households

   d. How can you use the information in parts (a)–(c) to find the mean?

B A group of seven students has a mean of three people per household.

   1. Make up a data set that fits this description.

   2. Make an ordered-value bar graph and a line or dot plot to represent your set of data.

   3. Describe how to use your bar graph to verify the mean is three people.

   4. Suppose you found another data set with seven households and a mean of three people per household, but with a greater range. How would this change the appearance of your line or dot plot?

   5. Explain how you can find the following on your graphs:

   a. each person's household size

   b. the total number of households

   c. the total number of people in the combined households

   d. How can you use the information in parts (a)–(c) to find the mean?

continued on the next page >

Problem **2.2** *continued*

C A group of six students has a mean of $3\frac{1}{2}$ people.

1. Make up a data set that fits this description.

2. Make an ordered-value bar graph and a line or dot plot to represent your set of data.

3. How can the mean be $3\frac{1}{2}$ people when "half" a person does not exist?

D The dot plot below shows the household sizes for a group of eight students.

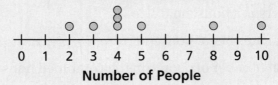

Household Size 3

Number of People

1. Identify the median, mode, and range of the distribution.

2. Think about viewing the distribution on a balance. Make an estimate or guess about where the mean is located.

3. Identify the mean of the distribution. How does this compare with your estimate or guess? Explain.

4. **a.** Compare the three measures of center—mean, median, and mode. How are they the same or different? Explain.

   b. Is it possible to have the three measures of center of a distribution all be the same? All be different? Explain.

   c. Which measure would you choose to describe the typical household size for the eight households? Explain.

E Look back at the work you did in Questions A–D and in Problem 2.1. Describe a method to compute the mean in any situation.

ACE Homework starts on page 48.

2.3 Making Choices
Mean or Median?

When you gather data about the typical middle-school student, you may want to inquire about what interests students have. In Problem 2.3, you will use data about skateboard prices to investigate when to use the mean or median to describe what is "typical."

Problem 2.3

The table below shows prices of skateboards at four different stores.

Retail Table 1: Prices of Skateboards (dollars)

Store A	Store B	Store C	Store D
60	13	40	179
40	40	20	160
13	45	60	149
45	60	35	149
20	50	50	149
30	30	30	145
35	15	13	149
60	35	45	100
50	15	40	179
70	70	50	145
50	50	60	149
50	70	70	149
60	50	70	149
50	10	50	149
35	120	90	145
15	90	120	150
70	120	120	149
120		200	149

continued on the next page >

Problem 2.3 *continued*

A The dot plots below show the data from Stores B and C.

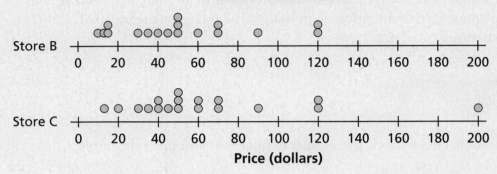

Skateboard Prices

1. Compute the median and mean of the data from the two stores.

2. For each store,

• Describe how the measures of center and dot plots are related.

• Describe how the distribution of the data influences the location of the mean and the median.

B Use the information in Retail Table 1.

1. Make a line plot showing the data from Store A.

2. Compute the mean and the median of Store A's prices.

3. Store A decides to stock some higher-priced skateboards. Using a different color, include these data values one at a time on your line plot. After you include each value, find the new mean and the new median of the data. Complete a copy of the table below.

Store A's New Stock

New Stock Price	New Mean	New Median
$200	■	■
$180	■	■
$180	■	■
$160	■	■
$170	■	■
$140	■	■

Problem **2.3** *continued*

4. Suppose the price of the last skateboard were $200, not $140. What would happen to the mean? To the median?

5. When do additional data values influence the mean of the distribution? Influence the median?

6. Which measure of center would you use to answer the question "What is the typical price of skateboards at Store A when all the higher-priced skateboards are included?" Explain your reasoning.

C Each dot plot below shows combined data for two stores from Retail Table 1. For one set of combined data, the mean is $107.11 and the median is $132.50. For the other set of combined data, the mean is $50.17 and the median is $50.00.

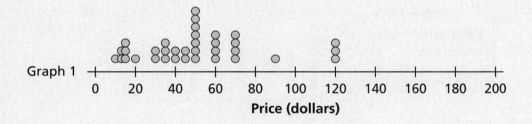

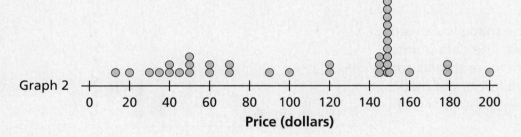

1. Write a complete title for each dot plot by identifying the two sets of data it shows. For example, *Graph 1: Skateboard Prices From Stores __?__ and __?__*. Explain your reasoning.

2. For one graph, the mean and median are almost the same. For the other, the mean and median are different. Explain how the distribution of the data influences the location of the mean or the median.

D In a blog, Dr. Statistics says that "the median is a resistant measure of center, and the mean is *not* a resistant measure of center." Explain the meaning of this statement using your results from Questions A–C.

continued on the next page >

Problem **2.3** | *continued*

E A distribution's shape can help you see trends in the data. The shape is **symmetric** if the data are spread out evenly around a center value. The shape is right- or left-**skewed** if the points cluster at one end of the graph.

Three groups of middle-school students were asked: "Using a scale of 1 to 10 (with 10 being the best), how would you rate skateboarding as a sport?" The dot plots below show the responses.

1. Find the mean and median marked on each dot plot. Describe how the measures are influenced, or not, by the shape of the distribution.

2. Describe how the students in each group feel about skateboarding. Which measure of center would you use to answer the question: "What is the students' typical rating?" Explain.

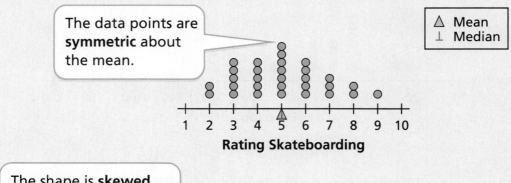

The data points are **symmetric** about the mean.

△ Mean
⊥ Median

Rating Skateboarding

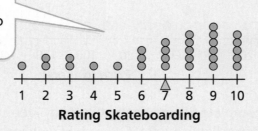

The shape is **skewed left**. The data points are more spread out to the left of the median.

Rating Skateboarding

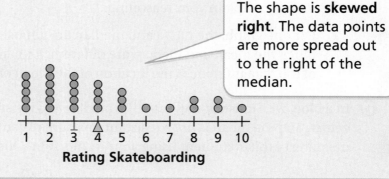

The shape is **skewed right**. The data points are more spread out to the right of the median.

Rating Skateboarding

A C E Homework starts on page 48.

2.4 Who Else Is in Your Household?
Categorical and Numerical Data

Some statistical questions have answers that are words or categories. For example, "What is your favorite sport?" has answers that are words. Other questions have answers that are numbers. For example, "How many inches tall are you?" has answers that are numbers.

Categorical data can be grouped into categories, such as "favorite sport." They are usually not numbers. Suppose you asked people how they got to school or what kinds of pets they had. Their answers would be categorical data.

Numerical data are counts or measures. Suppose you asked people how tall they were or how many pets they had. Their responses would be numerical data.

* Which questions below have words or categories as answers? Which have numbers as answers?

One middle-school class gathered data about their pets by tallying students' responses to these questions:

- How many pets do you have?
- What is your favorite kind of pet?

The students made tables to show the tallies, or frequencies. Then they made bar graphs to show the data distributions.

Number of Pets

Number	0	1	2	3	4	5	6	7	8	9	10	11	12	13	14	15	16	17	18	19	20	21
Frequency	2	2	5	4	1	2	3	0	1	1	0	0	1	0	1	0	0	1	0	1	0	1

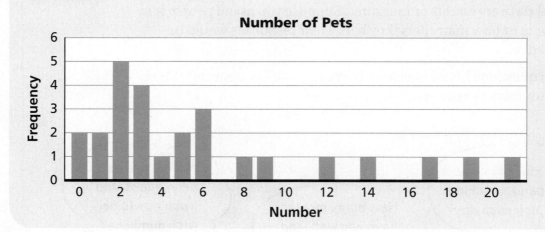

Favorite Pet

Pet	Frequency
cat	4
dog	7
fish	2
bird	2
horse	3
goat	1
cow	2
rabbit	3
duck	1
pig	1

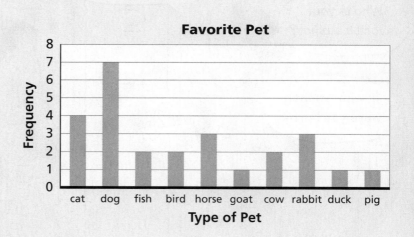

Problem 2.4

Decide whether Questions A through E can be answered by using data from the graphs and tables. If so, give the answer and explain how you got it. If not, explain why not.

A Which graph shows categorical data? Numerical data?

B   **1.** What is the total number of pets the students have?

    2. What is the greatest number of pets a student has?

C   **1.** How many students are in the class?

    2. How many students chose a cat as their favorite kind of pet?

    3. How many cats do students have as pets?

D   **1.** What is the mode of the favorite kind of pet? The mean?

    2. What is the median number of pets students have? The range?

E   **1.** Tomas is a student in this class. How many pets does he have?

    2. Do the girls in the class have more pets than the boys?

F Using the distribution of the data, how would you describe the number of pets owned by this class? What would you say were the favorite kinds of pets? Use measures of center and other tools to help you describe the results of the survey.

A C E Homework starts on page 48.

Did you know?

Goldfish are trainable. With coaching, goldfish can learn to swim through hoops and tunnels, push a tiny ball into a net, and pull a lever for food.

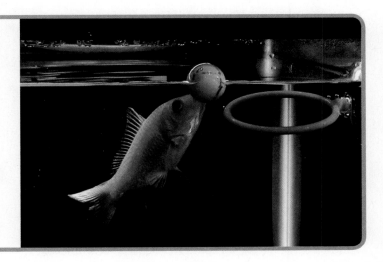

Applications

For Exercises 1–3, use the line plot below.

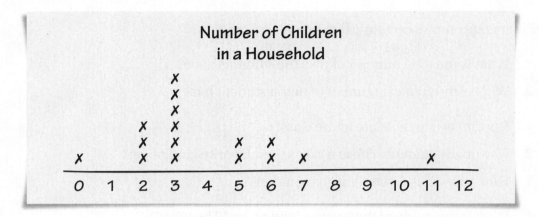

1. a. What is the median number of children in the 16 households? Explain how to find the median. What does the median tell you?

   b. Do any of the 16 households have the median number of children? Explain why this is possible.

2. a. What is the mean number of children per household for the 16 households? Explain how to find the mean. What does the mean tell you?

   b. Do any of the 16 households have the mean number of children? Explain why this is possible.

3. Use either the mean or the median to answer this question: "What is the typical household size for the data?" Explain your reasoning.

For Exercises 4–7, the mean number of people per household in eight households is six people.

4. **Multiple Choice** What is the total number of people in the eight households?

   A. 16   **B.** 64   **C.** 14   **D.** 48

5. Make a line plot showing one possible arrangement of the numbers of people in the eight households.

6. Make a line plot showing a different possible arrangement of the numbers of people in the eight households.

7. Are the medians the same for the two distributions you made? Is it possible to have two distributions that have the same means, but not the same medians? Explain your reasoning.

8. A set of nine households has a mean of $3\frac{1}{3}$ people per household. Make a line plot showing a data set that fits this description.

9. A set of nine households has a mean of five people per household. The largest household in the group has ten people. Make a line plot showing a data set that fits this description.

For Exercises 10–16, tell whether the answers to the question are numerical or categorical data.

10. What is your height in centimeters?

11. What is your favorite musical group?

12. In which month were you born?

13. What would you like to do when you graduate from high school?

14. Use your foot as a unit of measure. How many of your "feet" tall are you?

15. What kind(s) of transportation do you use to get to school?

16. On average, how much time do you spend doing homework each day?

Connections

17. During Mr. Wilson's study hall, students spent the following amounts of time on their homework:

$\frac{3}{4}$ hour $\frac{1}{2}$ hour $1\frac{1}{4}$ hours $\frac{3}{4}$ hour $\frac{1}{2}$ hour

a. What is the mean time Mr. Wilson's students spent on homework?

b. Multiple Choice What is the median time the students spent on homework?

  F. $\frac{1}{2}$ hour   **G.** $\frac{3}{4}$ hour

  H. 1 hour   **J.** $1\frac{1}{4}$ hours

18. A soccer league wants to find the average amount of water its players drink per game. There are 18 players on a team. During one game, the two teams drank a total of 1,152 ounces of water.

a. How much water did each player drink per game if each player drank the same amount of water?

b. Does this value represent the mean or the median? Explain.

19. Sabrina, Diego, and Marcus entered a Dance-a-thon that ran from 9 A.M. to 7 P.M. The times that each student danced are shown at the right.

a. Write the number of hours each student spent dancing as a mixed number.

b. Look at the data from part (a). Without doing any computations, do you think the mean time spent dancing is the same as, less than, or greater than the median? Explain.

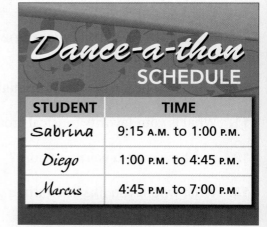

Dance-a-thon SCHEDULE

STUDENT	TIME
Sabrina	9:15 A.M. to 1:00 P.M.
Diego	1:00 P.M. to 4:45 P.M.
Marcus	4:45 P.M. to 7:00 P.M.

20. Jon has a pet rabbit that is 5 years old. He wonders if his rabbit is old compared to other rabbits. At the pet store, he finds out that the mean life span for a rabbit is 7 years.

  a. What does the mean tell Jon about the life span for a rabbit?

  b. What additional information would help Jon to predict the life span of his rabbit?

21. A store carries nine different brands of granola bars. What are possible prices for each of the nine brands of granola bars if the mean price is $1.33? Explain how you determined values for each of the nine brands. You may use pictures to help you.

For Exercises 22–25, a recent survey of 25 students in a middle-school class yielded the data in the table below.

Mean Time Spent on Leisure Activities by Students in One Class

Activity	Time (minutes per day)
Watching videos	39
Listening to music	44
Using the computer	21

22. Did each student watch videos for 39 minutes per day? Explain.

23. Jill decides to round 39 minutes to 40 minutes. Then she estimates that the students spend about $\frac{2}{3}$ of an hour watching videos. What percent of an hour is $\frac{2}{3}$?

24. Estimate what part of an hour the students spend listening to music. Write your answer as a fraction and as a decimal.

25. The students spend about 20 minutes per day using a computer. How many hours do they spend using a computer in 1 week (7 days)? Write your answer as a fraction and as a decimal.

26. Three candidates are running for the mayor of Slugville. Each has determined the typical income of residents of Slugville, and they use that information for campaign sound bites.

Some of the candidates are confused about "average." Slugville has only 16 residents. Their weekly incomes are $0, $0, $0, $0, $0, $0, $0, $0, $200, $200, $200, $200, $200, $200, $200, and $30,600.

a. Explain what measure of center each of the candidates used as an "average" income for the town. Check their computations.

b. Does anyone in Slugville have the mean income? Explain.

c. Does anyone in Slugville have an income that equals the median? Explain.

d. Does anyone in Slugville have an income that equals the mode? Explain.

e. When you decide to use a measure of center—mode, median, or mean—you must choose which measure best helps you tell the story of the data. What do you consider to be the typical income for a resident of Slugville? Explain your choice of measure.

f. Suppose four more people moved to Slugville. Each has a weekly income of $200. How would the mean, median, and mode change?

27. A recent survey asked 25 middle-school students how many movies they see in one month. The table and line plot below show the data.

Movies Watched in One Month

Student	Number	Student	Number	Student	Number
Wes	2	Susan	4	Julian	2
Tomi	15	Gil	3	Alana	4
Ling	13	Enrique	2	Tyrone	1
Su Chin	1	Lonnie	3	Rebecca	4
Michael	9	Ken	10	Anton	11
Mara	30	Kristina	15	Jun	8
Alan	20	Mario	12	Raymond	8
Jo	1	Henry	5	Anjelica	17
Tanisha	25				

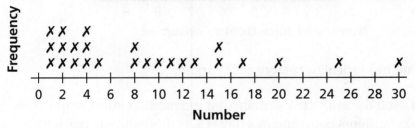

Movies Watched in One Month

a. Identify one section of the line plot where about half the data values are grouped and a different section where about one quarter of the data is grouped.

b. What is the range of the data? Explain how you found it.

c. Find the mean number of movies watched by the students. Explain.

d. What do the range and mean tell you about the typical number of movies watched for this group of students?

e. Find the median number of movies watched. Are the mean and the median the same? Why do you think this is so?

For Exercises 28–32, use the graph below. The graph shows the number of juice drinks 100 middle-school students consumed in one day.

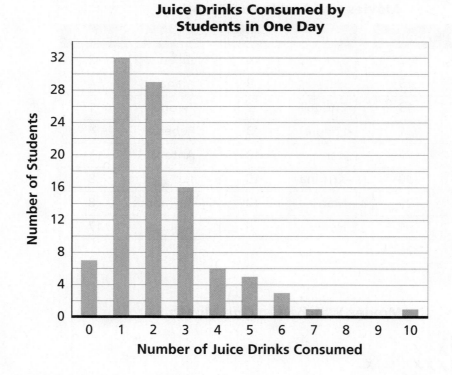

Juice Drinks Consumed by Students in One Day

28. Are the data numerical or categorical? Explain.

29. A student used the graph to estimate that the median number of juice drinks students consume in a day is 5. Is this estimate correct? Explain your answer.

30. Another student estimates that the median number of juice drinks is 1. Is this estimate correct? Explain your answer.

31. What is the total number of juice drinks these 100 students consume in one day? How did you determine your answer?

32. Suppose the survey had asked, "What juice drinks do you like?"

   a. List three possible responses.

   b. Are the data numerical or categorical? Explain.

   c. Describe how to make a bar graph showing the distribution of the data collected in answer to this question. How would you label the horizontal axis? The vertical axis? How would you title the graph? What would each bar on the graph show?

Extensions

For Exercises 33 and 34, use the newspaper headlines.

OUR TOWN TIMES

How Much Screen Time Is Too Much?

Students Spend 900 Hours a Year in School.

Students Spend 1,170 Hours on TV and Internet.

33. Do you think that each headline refers to a mean, a median, or something else? Explain.

34. About how many hours per day does the average sixth grader spend watching television or using the Internet if he or she spends 1,170 hours of screen time in a year?

For Exercises 35–37, use the table at the right.

35. Make a bar graph to display the data. Think about how you will set up and label the horizontal and vertical axes with the correct scales.

36. Use the information in your graph to write a paragraph about the pets these students own. How do these results compare to the results from the class data used in Problem 2.4?

37. Estimate how many students were surveyed. Explain your reasoning.

Types of Pets Students Own

Pet	Frequency
bird	61
cat	184
dog	180
fish	303
gerbil	17
guinea pig	12
hamster	32
horse	28
rabbit	2
snake	9
turtle	13
Total	**841**

In this Investigation, you explored a measure of center called the mean. It is important to understand how the mean, or average, is related to the mode and the median. The following questions will help you summarize what you learned.

Think about these questions. Discuss your ideas with other students and your teacher. Then write a summary of your findings in your notebook.

1. **Describe** a method for calculating the mean of a set of data. Explain why your method works.

2. You have used three measures of center—mode, median, and mean—to describe distributions.

   a. **Why** do you suppose they are called "measures of center"?

   b. **What** does each tell you about a set of data?

   c. **How** do you decide which measure of center to use when describing a distribution?

   d. **Why** might you want to include both the range and a measure of center when reporting a statistical summary?

3. a. One student says you can only use the mode to describe categorical data, but you can use the mode, median, and mean to describe numerical data. Is the student correct? Explain.

   b. Can you find the range for categorical data? Explain.

Unit Project

Think about the survey you will be developing to gather information about middle-school students.

 How might the new ideas you have learned in this Investigation be useful when you are designing a statistical analysis?

Common Core Mathematical Practices

As you worked on the Problems in this Investigation, you used prior knowledge to make sense of them. You also applied your Mathematical Practices to solve the Problems. Think back over your work, the ways you thought about the Problems, and how you used Mathematical Practices.

Sophie described her thoughts in the following way:

If a set of seven numbers has a mean of 11, then the sum of the numbers is going to equal 77—no matter what.

For example, the set of numbers 5, 9, 9, 9, 12, 15, and 18 has a mean of 11 and a sum of 77. Another set of numbers, 4, 5, 6, 10, 10, 11, and 31, has a mean of 11. That set of numbers also has a sum of 77.

I can just replace each of the original seven numbers with the number 11, just like evening out the cube stacks. And when I add 11 seven times, the sum is 77.

Common Core Standards for Mathematical Practice

MP7 Look for and make use of structure

- What other Mathematical Practices can you identify in Sophie's reasoning?

- Describe a Mathematical Practice that you and your classmates used to solve a different Problem in this Investigation.

What's Your Favorite...? Measuring Variability

 A statistical investigation begins by asking a question. Decisions about what data to collect are based on the question.

When people collect answers to a question, the data may be similar, such as the number of raisins found in each of 30 different half-ounce boxes of raisins. More often, however, the data vary, such as the pulse rates of 30 different people after each person rides a roller coaster.

When you are interested in learning about a person, you may ask a question that begins "What is your favorite . . .?" For example, you might ask "What is your favorite cereal?"

WHEATY O's
serving size
$\frac{3}{4}$ cup or 28 grams

Honey Clouds
serving size
1 cup or 30 grams

RAISIN flakes
serving size
$1\frac{1}{4}$ cups or 33 grams

Fruity Crisps
serving size
$\frac{3}{4}$ cup or 30 grams

Common Core State Standards

6.SP.A.1 Recognize a statistical question as one that anticipates variability in the data related to the question and accounts for it in the answers.

6.SP.A.3 Recognize that a measure of center for a numerical data set summarizes all of its values with a single number, while a measure of variation describes how its values vary with a single number.

Also 6.RP.A.3, 6.RP.A.3a, 6.NS.C.6, 6.NS.C.7, 6.SP.A.2, 6.SP.B.4, 6.SP.B.5c, 6.SP.B.5d

The graph below shows the results of an online survey of 4,500 people. Each person took the survey once.

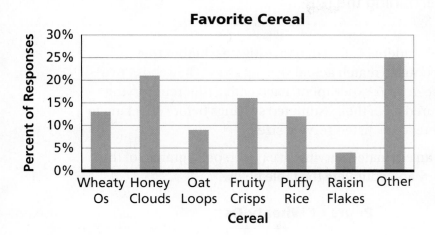

- What do you know about cereal choices from this survey?

You can investigate other information related to cereal. For example, a recent report claims that children "overpour" their cereal, meaning they pour portions that are larger than a single serving size. This is a problem because many cereals have high sugar contents.

- Do you think that children overpour by the same amount for all cereals? Explain.

Understanding and explaining variability in data is the essence of statistical problem solving. **Variability** in numerical data indicates how spread out a distribution of data is. One way to compare data distributions is to describe which data set is *more variable* (spread out) or *less variable* (clustered together). In this Investigation, you will learn some other ways to describe how data vary.

3.1 Estimating Cereal Serving Sizes
Determining the IQR

Twelve middle-school students decided to investigate whether they could pour cereal portions to match actual serving sizes. They chose two different cereals to use in their experiment, each with a different serving size. The students poured all of their estimated servings before checking to see how close they were to the listed serving sizes.

Each student poured an estimated serving size ($\frac{3}{4}$ cup or 28 grams) of the cereal Wheaty Os. Copy and complete the table below.

Pours of Wheaty Os

Grams Poured	52	29	32	59	43	24	28	23	20	30	37	27
Serving Size	1.86	1.04	1.14	▨	▨	0.86	▨	0.82	0.71	1.07	▨	0.96

- How could you compute the data values in the serving-size row?

The dot plot below shows the distribution of the serving-size data. The data values you calculated to complete the table are already included.

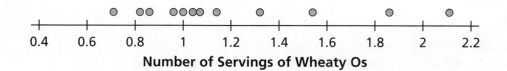

0.4　　0.6　　0.8　　1　　1.2　　1.4　　1.6　　1.8　　2　　2.2

Number of Servings of Wheaty Os

- Which measure of center—mean, median, or mode—might you use to describe a typical serving size poured by the students?

- How well do you think students estimated the serving size when they poured Wheaty Os?

You have already learned how to find the median of a data set. In Problem 3.1, you will work with values called **quartiles**—the three points that divide an ordered set of data into four equal groups, with each group containing one-fourth of the data values.

Problem 3.1

A The students agreed that being "about right" means pouring a serving size that is in the middle 50% of the data distribution. The students arranged the twelve Wheaty Os data values in order from least to greatest on sticky notes.

| 0.71 | 0.82 | 0.86 | 0.96 | 1.00 | 1.04 | 1.07 | 1.14 | 1.32 | 1.54 | 1.86 | 2.11 |

1. What is the median?

2. Identify the **lower quartile** (Q1). Its *position* is located midway between the serving sizes 0.86 and 0.96. Find the *value* of the lower quartile.

3. Identify the **upper quartile** (Q3). Its *position* is located midway between the serving sizes 1.32 and 1.54. Find the *value* of the upper quartile.

4. How are the positions of Q1 and Q3 related to the position of the median (sometimes called Q2)?

5. The serving size estimates between Q1 and Q3 are in the middle 50% of the data. Do you agree that serving size estimates in the middle 50% are "about right"? Explain.

6. The **interquartile range (IQR)** is the difference Q3 – Q1. The IQR measures the *spread* of the middle 50% of the data. What is the IQR for the Wheaty Os data?

continued on the next page >

Problem **3.1** *continued*

B The students also poured estimated servings ($1\frac{1}{4}$ cup or 33 grams) of Raisin Flakes.

1. On a copy of the table below, write the serving sizes of the data they gathered.

Pours of Raisin Flakes

Grams Poured	44	33	31	24	42	31	28	24	15	36	30	41
Serving Size	1.33	1.00	■	■	■	0.94	■	■	■	1.09	■	■

2. Make a line plot or a dot plot to show the frequency of the distribution of data values. Use the same number-line labels as the Wheaty Os dot plot at the beginning of Investigation 3.

3. Arrange the data in order from least to greatest. What is the median?

4. Find Q1 and Q3. Use these to identify the middle 50% of the data.

5. Describe the estimated servings that are in the middle 50% of the distribution. Do you agree that the estimated servings in the middle 50% are "about right"? Explain.

6. Calculate the IQR of the estimated servings of Raisin Flakes. Explain how you found this number.

C Use the interquartile ranges of the Wheaty Os and Raisin Flakes data.

1. For which cereal are the data more spread out? Explain.

2. Is IQR a good measure of whether students consistently underpour or overpour cereal servings? Explain.

3. How would you describe a typical serving of Wheaty Os as poured by the students? Of Raisin Flakes?

Problem 3.1 *continued*

D Recall that the range of a data set is a measure of variability (or spread).

    1. Compute the range of the Wheaty Os data. Compute the range of the Raisin Flakes data.

    2. What do the ranges tell you about how the poured servings vary? Explain.

    3. Compare the ranges and the IQRs of each data set. How are they alike? How are they different?

E Each student wrote a report comparing the two data sets. Two students, Seamus and Deanna, gave the answers below. Do you agree with Seamus or with Deanna? Explain your reasoning.

Seamus

For servings of Raisin Flakes, both the range (0.88 g) and the IQR (0.375 g) are less than the range (1.4 g) and IQR (0.52 g) of Wheaty Os.

About one third of the students overpoured the servings of Raisin Flakes (33 g), but almost two thirds of the students overpoured the servings of Wheaty Os (38 g). Students seem more accurate at estimating servings of Raisin Flakes.

Deanna

The median serving size poured for the Raisin Flakes data is 0.94 of a serving. The median serving size poured for the Wheaty Os data is 1.055 of a serving. Students seem to overpour Wheaty Os and underpour Raisin Flakes.

 Homework starts on page 72.

3.2 Connecting Cereal Shelf Location and Sugar Content

Describing Variability Using the IQR

Cereal boxes have nutritional information on the side panel. Sugar content is reported in grams per serving.

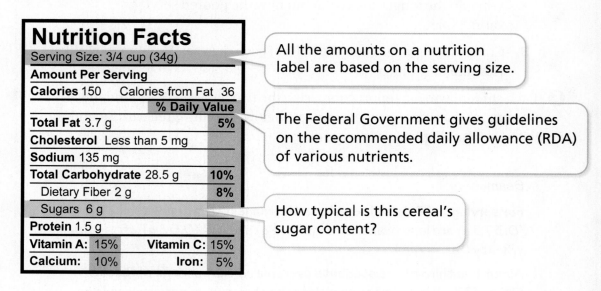

Nutrition Facts

Serving Size: 3/4 cup (34g)

Amount Per Serving

Calories 150   Calories from Fat 36

	% Daily Value
Total Fat 3.7 g	5%
Cholesterol Less than 5 mg	
Sodium 135 mg	
Total Carbohydrate 28.5 g	10%
Dietary Fiber 2 g	8%
Sugars 6 g	
Protein 1.5 g	
Vitamin A: 15% **Vitamin C:** 15%	
Calcium: 10% **Iron:** 5%	

All the amounts on a nutrition label are based on the serving size.

The Federal Government gives guidelines on the recommended daily allowance (RDA) of various nutrients.

How typical is this cereal's sugar content?

The dot plot below shows the distribution of grams of sugar per serving for 70 cereals. The median is 7.5 grams of sugar, or about 2 teaspoons of sugar, per serving. The red marker (⊥) indicates the median.

Distribution of Sugar in 70 Cereals

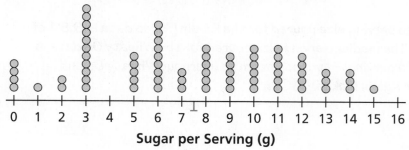

Sugar per Serving (g)

- What surprises you about the data set or its distribution? Explain.
- What questions do you have as you look at the distribution?

You have used two measures of variability: range and interquartile range
(IQR). In Problem 3.2, you will use the IQR to describe variability in grams
of sugar for different groups of cereals.

Problem 3.2

A Use the dot plot on the previous page showing the distribution of sugar
in cereals.

  1. Are there intervals where the data cluster? What does this tell you
  about the data?

  2. The table below shows some of the data. On a copy of the dot plot
  from the previous page, locate each data point.

Distribution of Sugar in Several Cereals

Cereals From Data Set	Sugar (grams)	Shelf Location
Bran-ful	5	Bottom
Crispy Bran	6	Top
Wheaty Os	1	Top
Fruity Crisps	13	Middle
Sugary Flakes	11	Top
Frosted Bites	7	Middle
Healthy Nuggets	3	Bottom
Honey Oats	6	Middle
Honey Wheaty Os	10	Top
Raisin Flakes	14	Middle

continued on the next page >

continued

B The dot plots below show data for the 70 cereals organized by supermarket shelf location.

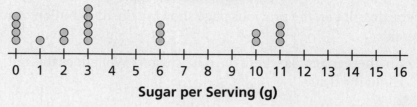

Sugar in Top-Shelf Cereals

Sugar per Serving (g)

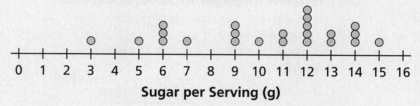

Sugar in Middle-Shelf Cereals

Sugar per Serving (g)

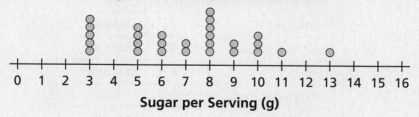

Sugar in Bottom-Shelf Cereals

Sugar per Serving (g)

1. Is there any pattern to how sugary a cereal is and its shelf location? Find ways to describe and compare the three distributions of data.

2. **a.** Find the IQR for each distribution.

   b. Which of the three distributions has the greatest variability in grams of sugar per serving? The least variability?

3.2 continued

3. Write a report comparing the cereals located on each of the shelves. Your report should

- use a measure of center to describe the typical number of grams of sugar in the cereals on each shelf.

- use a measure of spread to describe the variability in the number of grams of sugar in the cereals on each shelf.

- compare the distributions of grams of sugar in the cereals on each of the three shelves by using the measures of center and spread above.

- point out anything unusual or interesting.

A C E Homework starts on page 72.

3.3 Is It Worth the Wait?
Determining and Describing Variability Using the MAD

In your lifetime, you spend a lot of time waiting. Sometimes it feels like you could stand in line forever. For example, you may wait a long time for your favorite ride at an amusement park.

During the summer, one estimate of average wait time at an amusement park is 60 minutes. The most popular rides can accommodate 1,500 people per hour. Lines form when more people arrive than the rides can fit. Amusement parks are designed to minimize wait times, but variability in the number of people who choose a particular ride can result in lines.

Sally and her family spent the day at an amusement park. At the end of the day, Sally noticed the sign below.

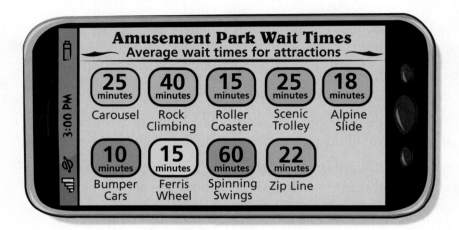

- Which ride has the shortest average wait time? The longest?

- Sally waited in line longer than 25 minutes for the Scenic Trolley ride. How could this have happened?

In Investigation 2, you learned that it is possible for a data set to include values that are quite different from the mean. In Problem 3.3, you will find a way to describe *how much* data values vary from an average.

Problem 3.3

A Since Sally waited in line longer than the average wait time, she wondered how much wait times vary.

The dot plot below shows a distribution of ten wait times for the Scenic Trolley ride.

Scenic Trolley Wait Times

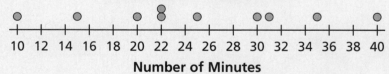

Number of Minutes

1. Sally says that the mean wait time is 25 minutes, just like the sign claimed. Do you agree? Explain.

Problem 3.3 continued

2. Sally wonders how typical a wait time of 25 minutes is. She says "I can find how much, on average, the data values vary from the mean time of 25 minutes." She uses the graph below to find the distance each data value is from the mean.

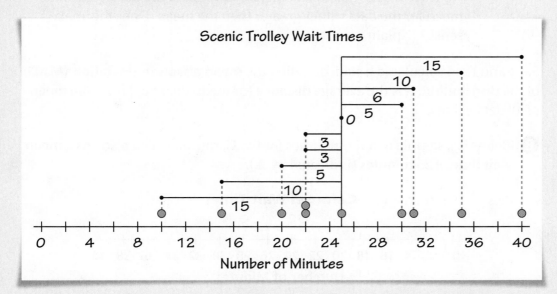

Fred says "That's a good idea, but I used an ordered-value bar graph to show the same idea."

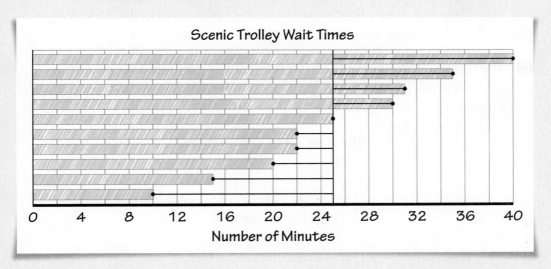

a. Describe how you can use each graph to find how much, on average, the data values vary from the mean time of 25 minutes.

continued on the next page >

Problem 3.3 *continued*

    b. What does this information tell you about how long you might have to wait in line to ride the Scenic Trolley?

    c. Sally noticed that the sum of the distances to the mean for the data values less than the mean equaled the sum of the distances to the mean for the data values greater than the mean. Does this make sense? Explain.

Sally and Fred calculated a statistic called the **mean absolute deviation (MAD)** of the distribution. It is the average distance (or mean distance) from the mean of all data values.

B   Below is a sample of ten wait times for the Carousel, which also has a mean wait time of 25 minutes (indicated by △).

Carousel Wait Times

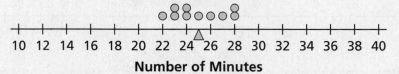

Number of Minutes

   1. Find the mean absolute deviation (MAD) for this distribution.

   2. Compare the MAD for the Scenic Trolley with the MAD for the Carousel. Why might you choose the Carousel over the Scenic Trolley? Explain.

C   The Bumper Cars have a mean wait time of 10 minutes. Like other rides, the wait times are variable. Below is a sample of ten wait times for the Bumper Cars.

Bumper Cars Wait Times

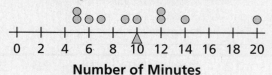

Number of Minutes

   1. What is the MAD for the Bumper Cars data?

   2. Compare the mean wait time of the Scenic Trolley and of the Bumper Cars. What do you notice? Then compare the MADs of both rides. What do you notice? Explain.

Problem **3.3** *continued*

D Use these two signs for amusement park rides. Suppose you have to leave the park in 30 minutes. You want one last ride. Each ride lasts 3 minutes. Which ride would you choose? Explain.

Average Wait Time: 18 minutes
MAD: 12 minutes

Average Wait Time: 22 minutes
MAD: 2 minutes

 Homework starts on page 72.

Applications

Servers at the Mugwump Diner receive tips for excellent service.

1. a. On Monday, four servers earned the tips below. Find the range of the tips.

b. The four servers shared their tips equally. How much money did each server get? Explain.

c. Yanna was busy clearing a table when the tips were shared. Yanna also received $16.10 in tips. Suppose Yanna's tips were included with the other tips, and the total was shared equally among the five servers. Without doing any computations, will the four servers receive less than, the same as, or more than they did before Yanna's tips were included? Explain.

2. On Tuesday, all five servers shared their tips equally. Each received $16.45. Does this mean someone originally received $16.45 in tips? Explain.

3. a. On Wednesday, Yanna received $13.40 in tips. When tips were shared equally among the five servers, each received $15.25. How could this have happened? Explain.

b. Based on the information in part (a), what can you say about the variability of the tip data on Wednesday? Explain your reasoning.

4. Recall the name-length data from Investigation 1. You explored name lengths from several different countries. The dot plots below show four distributions of data. Each dot plot shows the median (⊥).

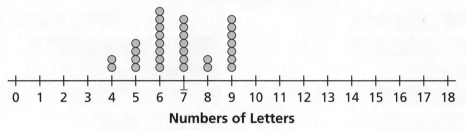

Chinese Pen-Pal Names

Numbers of Letters

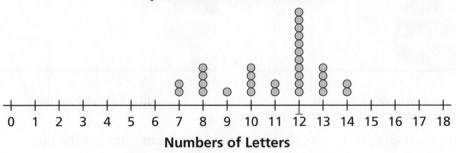

Japanese Pen-Pal Names

Numbers of Letters

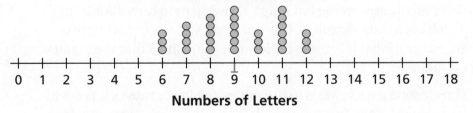

Korean Pen-Pal Names

Numbers of Letters

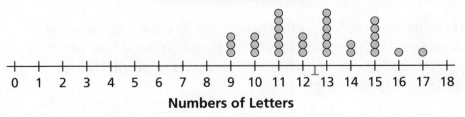

U.S. Student Names

Numbers of Letters

a. What is the interquartile range (IQR) of each distribution? Explain how you found each IQR.

b. Using the IQRs, for which distribution is the middle 50% the least spread out? The most spread out? Explain.

5. Below are two ordered-value bar graphs (Sample 1 and Sample 2), each showing nine households with a mean of five people per household.

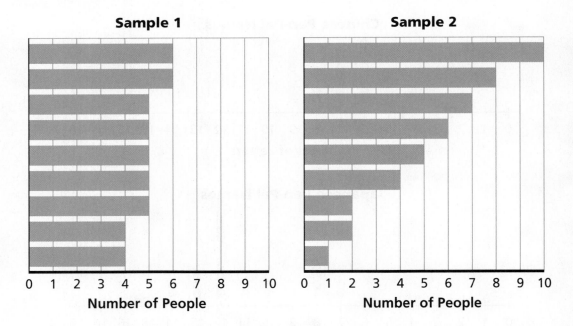

Sample 1

Sample 2

Number of People

Number of People

a. For each sample, how many *moves* does it take to even out the bars so that the mean is 5? A "move" is the movement of one person from one household to another household.

b. Draw an ordered-value bar graph showing nine households in which each data value is 5. Use the same scale as the other two graphs and label it Sample 3. How does this show that the mean is five people?

c. The closer a data value is to the mean, the fewer moves it takes to even out the data. In which graph (Sample 1, 2, or 3) are the data closest to the mean (vary the least)? Farthest from the mean (vary the most)? Explain.

d. Using the three ordered-value bar graphs, find the mean absolute deviation (MAD) for each set of data. Based on the MADs, which set of data varies the most from the mean of five people? Varies the least? Explain.

6. Jeff and Elaine are studying for their final exam. The grading spreadsheet below shows their practice-test scores. Each test has a top score of 100.

File	Edit	Tool	View	Chart	Class	Help

Algebra 1 Practice Tests | Algebra 1 Homework

Class	Name	Student Number	Test 1	Test 2	Test 3	Test 4	Test 5	Test 6	Test 7	Test 8	Test Average
001	Jeff	# 18	75	80	75	80	75	80	85	90	
001	Elaine	# 24	60	70	80	70	80	90	100	90	

Low Score [　　] | High Score [　　]

a. Make a line plot of each person's practice tests scores.

b. What are the median and IQR of each distribution?

c. What are the mean and MAD of each distribution?

d. On the day of the exam, who is more likely to receive a score of 80, Jeff or Elaine? Explain your reasoning.

7. The dot plots below show the distributions of ten wait times at two rides.

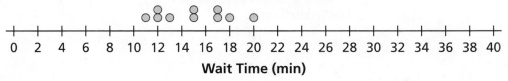

Amusement Park Ride 1

Wait Time (min)

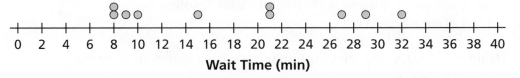

Amusement Park Ride 2

Wait Time (min)

a. Find the mean of each data set.

b. Compute the MAD of each data set.

c. Compare the MADs. In which distribution do the data vary more from the mean? Explain.

d. i. Make your own data set of ten wait times. Draw a dot plot.

  ii. Compute the MAD.

  iii. Compare the three distributions. In which distribution do the data vary more from the mean? Explain your thinking.

For Exercises 8–10, use the line plots below.

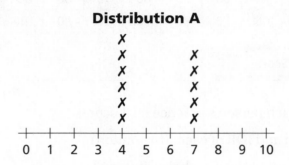

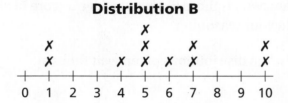

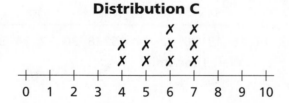

8. Find the interquartile range (IQR) and mean absolute deviation (MAD) of each data set.

9. Using the MAD, which distribution has the least variation from the mean? The most?

10. Using the IQR, which distribution has the greatest spread in the middle 50% of data? The least?

11. The frequency table below shows the number of pets owned by students in three different sixth-grade classes.

Pet Ownership

Number of Pets	Class 1	Class 2	Class 3
0	5	4	2
1	3	1	2
2	5	5	5
3	2	3	4
4	0	3	1
5	0	1	2
6	1	2	3
7	0	0	0
8	0	0	1
9	0	0	1
10	0	0	0
11	0	1	0
12	0	0	1
13	1	0	0
14	1	0	1
15	0	0	0
16	0	0	0
17	0	0	1
18	0	0	0
19	0	0	1
20	0	0	0
21	0	0	1
22	0	0	0
23	1	0	0
24	1	0	0

a. Draw a line plot or dot plot of each data set. Use the same scale on each graph so you can easily compare the distributions.

b. Compute the median and IQR for each distribution. Write at least three statements to compare the classes using the median and IQR.

c. Below are the means and MADs for each data set. Write at least three statements to compare the classes using the means and MADs.

Pet Ownership Statistics

Number of Pets	Class 1	Class 2	Class 3
Mean	5	2.67	6
MAD	3.6	1.74	4.46

Connections

For Exercises 12 and 13, use the bar graph below.

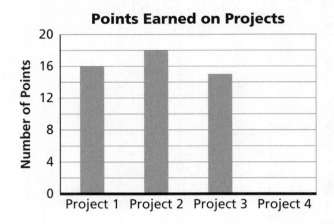

Points Earned on Projects

12. a. Malaika's mean score is 17 points. How many points did Malaika receive on Project 4? Explain.

b. What is the range of Malaika's scores on the four projects? What does this tell you about the variation in her scores?

13. Each project has a maximum score of 20 points.

a. What would Malaika's mean score be if she had a total of 80 points for the four projects? A total of 60 points?

b. Give four possible project scores that would result in each mean score in part (a).

c. What is the range of the scores for each of your sets of four project scores? What does this tell you about how spread out or variable the scores are?

d. Are these ranges more spread out, or variable, than the range of Malaika's set of scores? Explain.

For Exercises 14–16, use the tables below.

Caffeine Content of Selected Soda Drinks

Name	Caffeine in 8 Ounces (mg)
Soda A	38
Soda B	37
Soda C	27
Soda D	27
Soda E	26
Soda F	24
Soda G	21
Soda H	15
Soda J	23

Caffeine Content of Selected Other Drinks

Name	Caffeine in 8 Ounces (mg)
Energy Drink A	77
Energy Drink B	70
Energy Drink C	25
Energy Drink D	21
Iced Tea A	19
Iced Tea B	10
Coffee Drink	83
Hot Cocoa	2
Juice Drink	33

14. **a.** Find the mean and median amounts of caffeine in the soda drinks.

   b. Find the mean and median amounts of caffeine in the other drinks.

   c. Using parts (a) and (b), is it possible to say which type of drink—sodas or other drinks—has greater variability in caffeine content? Explain.

   d. Write three statements comparing the amounts of caffeine in sodas and other drinks.

15. Indicate whether each statement is true or false.

   a. Soda B has more caffeine than Soda F or Soda D.

   b. Energy Drink C has about three times as much caffeine per serving as Energy Drink A.

   c. 75% of all the drinks have 25 mg or less of caffeine per serving.

16. In Exercise 14, you found the means and medians of the sodas and the other drinks. Two MADs and two IQRs are listed below.

MAD = 5.16 mg   MAD = 25.93 mg
IQR = 10 mg   IQR = 59 mg

   a. Which statistics describe the variability of caffeine content in the sodas? Explain your reasoning.

   b. Which statistics describe the variability of caffeine content in the other drinks? Explain.

For Exercises 17 and 18, use the dot plots below.

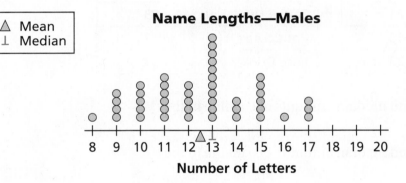

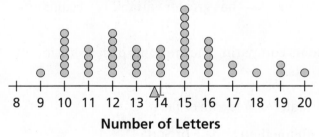

17. Compare the two sets of data. Which group has longer names? Explain.

18. Look at the distribution for females. Suppose that the data for four names with 18 or more letters changed. These students now have name lengths of ten or fewer letters.

   a. Draw a dot plot showing this change.

   b. Will the change affect the median name length for females? Explain.

   c. Will the change affect the mean name length for females? Explain.

19. Multiple Choice John's test scores were 100, 84, 88, 96, and 96. His teacher told him that his final grade is 96. Which measure of center did his teacher use to report John's final grade?

A. Mean   **B.** Median

C. Mode   **D.** Range

20. Multiple Choice Sal's Packages on the Go mails 6 packages with a mean weight of 7.1 pounds. Suppose the mean weight of five of these packages is 6.3 pounds. What is the weight of the sixth package?

F. 4.26 lb   **G.** 6.7 lb

H. 10.3 lb   **J.** 11.1 lb

21. Multiple Choice Which of the following is true about the IQR?

A. It describes the variability of the middle 50% of the data values.

B. It describes, on average, the distance of each data value from the mean.

C. It uses the minimum and maximum data value in its computation.

D. It is a statistic that is affected by extremely high values or extremely low values.

22. A gymnast receives the six scores below.

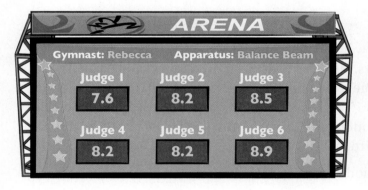

a. What is her mean score?

b. What happens to the mean when you multiply each data value by 2? By $\frac{2}{3}$? By 0.2?

c. Why does the mean change in each situation?

For Exercises 23–25, use the data below.

- Four pop songs have durations of 162, 151, 174, and 149 seconds.
- Four folk songs have durations of 121, 149, 165, and 184 seconds.

23. **Multiple Choice** What is the MAD of the folk songs' durations?

   F. 18 seconds   **G.** 19 seconds   **H.** 18.25 seconds   **J.** 19.75 seconds

24. **Multiple Choice** What is the MAD of the pop songs' durations?

   A. 2 seconds   **B.** 5 seconds   **C.** 6 seconds   **D.** 9 seconds

25. **Multiple Choice** Which of the following statements is true?

   F. The variability in folk songs' durations is about half that of pop songs.

   G. The variability in folk songs' durations is about twice that of pop songs.

   H. The variability in folk songs' durations is about three times that of pop songs.

   J. The variability in folk songs' durations is about four times that of pop songs.

Extensions

26. Mark has an easy way to find his mean test score: "Each math test is worth 100 points. Suppose I get 60 on my first test and 90 on my second. My average would be 75, because half of 60 is 30, half of 90 is 45, and 30 + 45 is 75. Now suppose I had three test scores: 60, 90, and 84. My average would be 78, because one third of 60 is 20, one third of 90 is 30, one third of 84 is 28, and 20 + 30 + 28 = 78."

    Does Mark's method always work? Explain.

27. Use the data set 20, 6, 10, 8, 12, 16, 14, 15, 14, 7.

    a. Find the mean, mode, and median. Then find the IQR and MAD.

    b. Add 3 to each data value in the set. Now determine the mean, mode, median, IQR, and MAD. What happened? Explain.

    c. Multiply each data value in the set by 2. Now determine the mean, mode, median, IQR, and MAD. What happened? Explain.

Mathematical Reflections 3

In this Investigation, you explored how data vary and how summary statistics can be used to describe variability. The following questions will help you summarize what you learned.

Think about your answers to these questions. Discuss your ideas with other students and your teacher. Then, write a summary of your findings in your notebook.

1. **Explain** and illustrate the following words.

   a. Range

   b. Interquartile range

   c. Mean absolute deviation

2. **a. Describe** how you can use the range to compare how two data distributions vary.

   b. Describe how you can use the IQR to compare how two data distributions vary.

   c. Describe how you can use the MAD to compare how two data distributions vary.

Unit Project

Think about the survey you will be developing to gather information about middle-school students.

 Will measures of variability, such as IQR and MAD, help you report observations about your data?

Common Core Mathematical Practices

As you worked on the Problems in this Investigation, you used prior knowledge to make sense of them. You also applied your Mathematical Practices to solve the Problems. Think back over your work, the ways you thought about the Problems, and how you used Mathematical Practices.

Shawna described her thoughts in the following way:

I figured out how to compare the IQR and the MAD. The IQR is related to the median. First, I find the median. Then, I find the midpoint of the data that are less than the median and the midpoint of the data that are greater than the median. The IQR is the difference of those two midpoints.

The MAD is related to the mean. First, I find the mean. Then I find the distance each data value is from the mean. To get an average deviation, I add up all the distances and divide the sum by the number of data values.

What this means is that the greater the IQR, the more the data vary from the median. The same goes for the MAD: The greater the MAD, the more the data vary from the mean.

Common Core Standards for Mathematical Practice
MP7 Look for and make use of structure

- What other Mathematical Practices can you identify in Shawna's reasoning?

- Describe a Mathematical Practice that you and your classmates used to solve a different Problem in this Investigation.

What Numbers Describe Us? Using Graphs to Group Data

People use numbers to describe a variety of attributes, or characteristics, of people, places, and things. These attributes include:

- activities, such as the amount of time it takes a student to get to school

- performances, such as the number of consecutive times a person can jump rope

- physical characteristics, such as a person's height

In this Investigation, you will examine graphs to identify patterns and trends in large sets of data. Grouping data before graphing makes the data easier to analyze. Your analysis can help you draw conclusions about the attribute being studied.

··

Common Core State Standards

6.SP.B.4 Display numerical data in plots on a number line, including dot plots, histograms, and box plots.

6.SP.B.5a Summarize numerical data sets in relation to their context, such as by reporting the number of observations.

6.SP.B.5c Summarize numerical data sets in relation to their context, such as by giving quantitative measures of center (median and/or mean) and variability (interquartile range and/or mean absolute deviation), as well as describing any overall pattern and any striking deviations from the overall pattern with reference to the context in which the data were gathered.

6.SP.B.5d Summarize numerical data sets in relation to their context, such as by relating the choice of measures of center and variability to the shape of the data distribution and the context in which the data were gathered.

Also 6.NS.C.6, 6.NS.C.7, 6.SP.A.1, 6.SP.A.2, 6.SP.A.3

4.1 Traveling to School
Histograms

A middle-school class studied the times that students woke up in the morning. They found that two students woke up almost an hour earlier than the others. The class wondered how much time it took each student to travel to school in the morning. The table below shows the data they collected.

- Based on the data, what three questions do you think the class asked?
- How might the class have collected the data?
- What information would a line plot of the data give you? A bar graph?

Students' Travel Times to School

Student	Travel Time (minutes)	Distance (miles)	Mode of Travel	Student	Travel Time (minutes)	Distance (miles)	Mode of Travel
LS	5	0.50	bus	DW	17	2.50	bus
CD	5	0.25	walking	MN	17	4.50	bus
ME	5	0.50	bus	AP	19	2.25	bus
EL	6	1.00	car	MP	20	1.50	bus
KR	8	0.25	walking	AT	20	2.75	bus
NS	8	1.25	car	JW	20	0.50	walking
NW	10	0.50	walking	JB	20	2.50	bus
RC	10	1.25	bus	MB	20	2.00	bus
JO	10	3.00	car	CF	20	1.75	bus
ER	10	1.00	bus	RP	21	1.50	bus
TH	11	1.50	bus	LM	22	2.00	bus
DD	15	2.00	bus	QN	25	1.50	bus
SE	15	0.75	car	AP	25	1.25	bus
AE	15	1.00	bus	CC	30	2.00	bus
CL	15	1.00	bus	BA	30	3.00	bus
HCP	15	1.50	bus	BB	30	4.75	bus
JW	15	1.50	bus	FH	35	2.50	bus
SW	15	2.00	car	KLD	35	0.75	bus
CW	15	2.25	bus	AB	50	4.00	bus
KG	15	1.75	bus	DB	60	4.50	bus

You can draw a histogram to display the data in the table. A **histogram** is a graph that organizes numerical data into *intervals*.

Step 1: Draw a dot plot or make a frequency table to display the data.

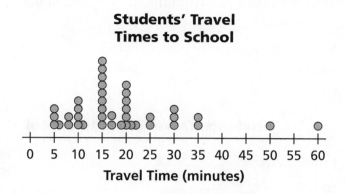

Students' Travel Times to School

Travel Time (minutes)

The data on student travel times vary from 5 minutes to 60 minutes.

• Why is the number line on the dot plot labeled every 5 minutes instead of every minute?

• How can you identify the data values of the dot plot when the number line is labeled every 5 minutes?

Step 2: Determine the frequency of the data values that fall into each interval, or group of consecutive numbers.

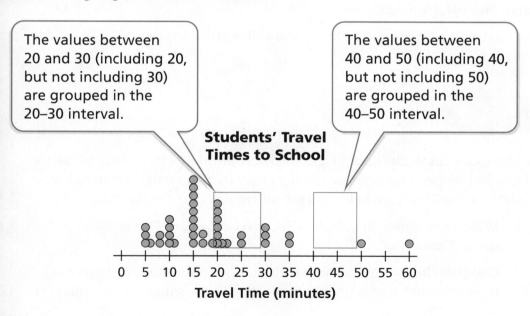

The values between 20 and 30 (including 20, but not including 30) are grouped in the 20–30 interval.

The values between 40 and 50 (including 40, but not including 50) are grouped in the 40–50 interval.

Students' Travel Times to School

Travel Time (minutes)

The height of each bar of the histogram represents the number of data values within a specified **interval**, or group of consecutive numbers.

Step 3: Draw the histogram. The histogram below has an interval size of 10 minutes.

Note: In the histogram below, data values of 10 minutes are graphed in the interval 10–20 minutes, data values of 20 minutes are graphed in the interval 20–30 minutes, and so on.

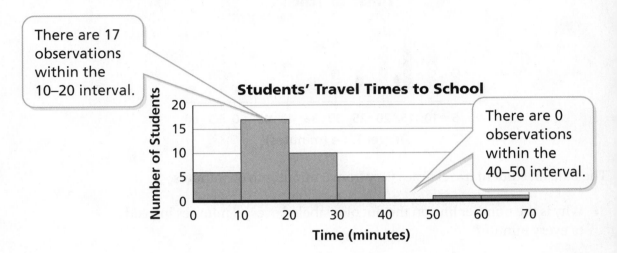

There are 17 observations within the 10–20 interval.

There are 0 observations within the 40–50 interval.

- How is a histogram like a bar graph? How is it different?
- How can you use a dot plot or a frequency table to help you make a histogram?
- What does *interval size* mean?
- Using the same data, what would a histogram with a different interval size look like?

Problem 4.1

In the histogram above, the data are grouped into 10-minute intervals. The data could also be grouped into larger or smaller intervals. Sometimes changing the interval size of the histogram helps you see different patterns in the data.

A 1. Make a histogram that displays the travel-time data. Use an interval size of 5 minutes.

2. Compare the histogram above with the histogram you drew in part (1). How does each histogram help you describe the student travel times?

B Which students most likely wake up the latest in the morning? Explain.

C Which students most likely wake up the earliest? Explain.

Data About Us

Problem 4.1 *continued*

D **1.** For the data on travel time, find the mode, the median, the mean, and the range. Explain how you found these statistics.

2. In what interval does the mode fall? The median? The mean?

E Which statistic, the mean or the median, would you choose to report when describing the average time it takes a student to travel to school? Explain.

A C E Homework starts on page 98.

4.2 Jumping Rope
Box-and-Whisker Plots

A **box-and-whisker plot,** or *box plot*, uses five statistical measures: the minimum data value, the lower quartile, the median, the upper quartile, and the maximum data value. These values separate a set of data into four groups with the same number of data values in each group.

The example below shows how these five statistics form a box plot.

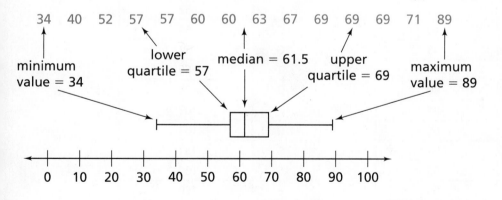

Two middle-school classes competed in a jumping-rope contest. The tables below show the data from each class.

Number of Consecutive Jumps, Mrs. R's Class

Gender	Number of Jumps
B	1
B	1
B	5
B	7
B	7
B	7
B	8
B	11
B	11
B	16
B	20
G	20
G	23
B	26
G	30
B	33
B	35
B	36
G	37
B	39
B	40
G	45
B	62
G	80
G	88
G	89
G	91
G	93
G	96
B	125

Number of Consecutive Jumps, Mr. K's Class

Gender	Number of Jumps
B	1
B	2
B	5
B	7
B	8
B	8
G	14
B	17
B	17
G	27
B	27
B	28
B	30
G	30
B	39
B	42
G	45
B	47
B	50
G	52
G	54
G	57
B	65
G	73
G	102
G	104
G	151
G	160
B	160
G	300

- Mr. K's class claims it is better at jumping rope than Mrs. R's class. What evidence might Mr. K's class be using?

The dot plots below show the distributions of the data from the tables.

- How are the dot plots similar? How are they different?

Consecutive Jumps by Mrs. R's Class

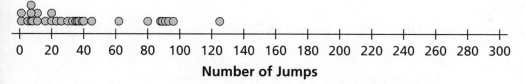

Number of Jumps

Consecutive Jumps by Mr. K's Class

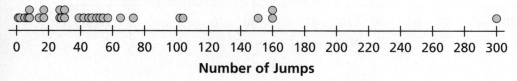

Number of Jumps

The minimum value (1), the lower quartile (17), the median (40.5), the upper quartile (65), and the maximum value (300) are shown on the dot plot below.

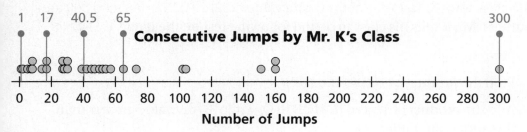

This box plot shows the same distribution of data as the dot plot above.

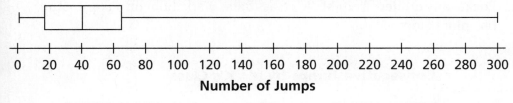

An **outlier** is an unusually high or low data value in a distribution. It could indicate that a value was recorded incorrectly. It could also indicate that the data value is unusual and is important to study.

- What values might be outliers in the data set for Mr. K's class?

- Look at the box-and-whisker plot. What is the typical number of jumps for a student in Mr. K's class? Explain your reasoning.

- Use what you know about box plots. Explain how box plots group a data distribution into quartiles, or four equal parts.

Problem 4.2

In this Problem, you will use box plots to compare data from the two classes.

A Use the dot plot below. Draw a box plot to display the data for Mrs. R's class.

Consecutive Jumps by Mrs. R's Class

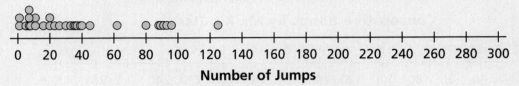

Number of Jumps

B Which class performed better in the jump-rope activity? Use information from the dot plots, box plots, and tables to explain your reasoning.

C Mr. K's class notices unusually high values in its class data. The students in the class want to test whether the data values 102, 104, 151, 160, and 300 are outliers. Mr. K tells his class to do the following test on the data:

- Find the IQR.

- Find the product of $1\frac{1}{2}$ and the IQR.

- Add the product of $1\frac{1}{2}$ and the IQR to Quartile 3. Any value greater than this sum is an outlier.

- Subtract the product of $1\frac{1}{2}$ and the IQR from Quartile 1. Any value less than this sum is an outlier.

 1. Locate any outliers from Mr. K's class data. Mark them on a copy of the box plot below.

Consecutive Jumps by Mr. K's Class

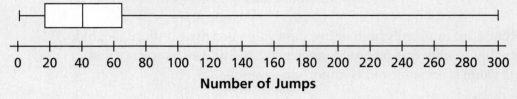

Number of Jumps

 2. Does Mrs. R's class data include outliers? Explain your reasoning. If Mrs. R's class data contains outliers, redraw your box plot to show which data values are outliers.

Problem **4.2** continued

D **1.** Calculate the mean of Mr. K's class data. Then calculate the mean and the median for Mr. K's class data without the outliers.

2. Do the outliers in Mr. K's class data have more of an effect on the median or on the mean? Explain.

3. Consider what you know about the outliers in the data. Does this change your answer to Question B? Explain.

E In Investigation 2, you used the words *symmetric* and *skewed* to describe the shapes of distributions. These descriptions can also be applied to distributions represented by box plots.

Below are three box plots. They show symmetric and skewed distributions.

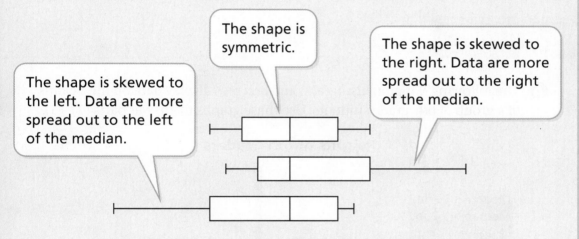

The shape is symmetric.

The shape is skewed to the right. Data are more spread out to the right of the median.

The shape is skewed to the left. Data are more spread out to the left of the median.

1. How does the location of the median in a box plot provide information about its shape?

2. How would you describe the shape of Mr. K's class data?

3. How would you describe the shape of Mrs. R's class data?

4. How does the shape of each distribution help you compare the two classes?

A **C** **E** Homework starts on page 98.

4.3 How Much Taller Is a 6th Grader Than a 2nd Grader?

Taking Variability Into Consideration

You can use various physical measures, such as height, to describe people. In this Problem, you will compare the heights of 6th-grade students and the heights of 2nd-grade students.

It is important to identify which graphs are most useful for answering different questions. You have used several types of graphs in this Unit: dot plots, line plots, histograms, and box plots. While answering the questions in this Problem, think about which graphs are most helpful.

- How much taller is a 6th grader than a 2nd grader?

Problem 4.3

A The following dot plot, histogram, and box plot display data on the heights of a group of 6th-grade students. Use these graphs to answer parts (1)–(5).

Heights of 6th Graders

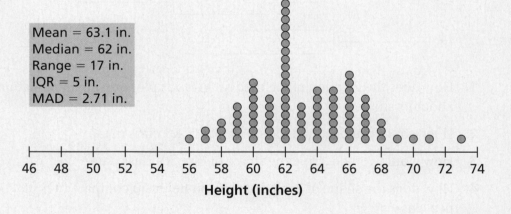

Mean = 63.1 in.
Median = 62 in.
Range = 17 in.
IQR = 5 in.
MAD = 2.71 in.

Height (inches)

Problem 4.3 continued

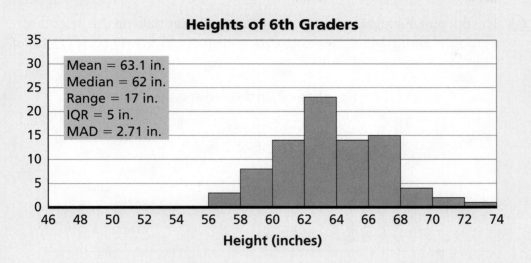

Heights of 6th Graders

Mean = 63.1 in.
Median = 62 in.
Range = 17 in.
IQR = 5 in.
MAD = 2.71 in.

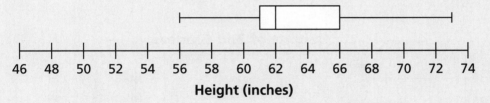

Heights of 6th Graders

1. Use one or more of the graphs to find the number of students in the group. Explain your reasoning.

2. What do you notice about the data values and their distribution? Explain which graph is most useful when describing the distribution.

3. Describe any clusters or gaps in the distribution. Explain which graph is most useful for identifying clusters or gaps.

4. Describe the spread of the distribution. Which data values occur frequently? Which data values occur infrequently? How close together are the data values? Explain which graph is most useful when describing how the data vary.

5. Describe how the dot plot, histogram, and box plot displaying the data are alike. Describe how they are different.

continued on the next page >

Problem 4.3 continued

B The dot plot, histogram, and box plot below display data on the heights of a group of 2nd-grade students. Use these displays to answer parts (1)–(5) of Question A for the 2nd-grade data.

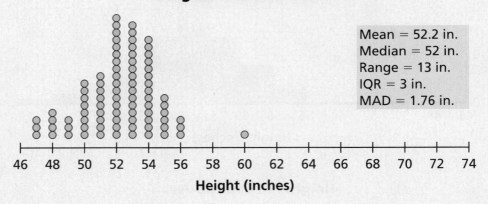

Heights of 2nd Graders

Mean = 52.2 in.
Median = 52 in.
Range = 13 in.
IQR = 3 in.
MAD = 1.76 in.

Height (inches)

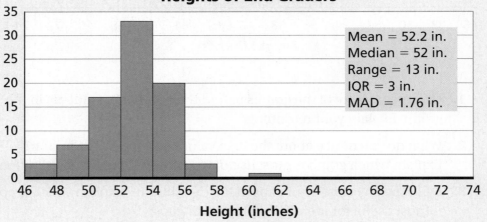

Heights of 2nd Graders

Mean = 52.2 in.
Median = 52 in.
Range = 13 in.
IQR = 3 in.
MAD = 1.76 in.

Height (inches)

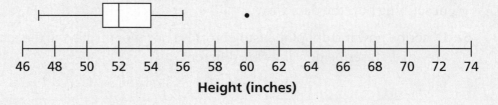

Heights of 2nd Graders

Height (inches)

Problem 4.3 continued

C Compare the graphs of the 6th-grade students to the graphs of the 2nd-grade students. For parts (1)–(4), consider the question below.

How much taller is a 6th-grade student than a 2nd-grade student?

1. Use the dot plots, means, and medians of both sets of data to answer the question. Explain your reasoning.

2. Use the histograms, means, and medians of both sets of data to answer the question. Explain your reasoning.

3. Use the box plots and medians of both sets of data to answer the question. Explain your reasoning.

4. Suppose you were writing a report to answer the question above. Which type of graphs would you choose to display? Explain.

D Use the range, IQR, and MAD for the 6th-grade and the 2nd-grade distributions. Is one distribution more spread out than the other? Explain.

E Suppose you were asked to write a report answering the question below. How would you collect data to answer the question? How would you display the data? What measures would you report?

How much taller is an 8th-grade student than a 6th-grade student?

A C E Homework starts on page 98.

Did You Know?

Head and Body Growth Over Time

Growth patterns in humans change over time. While people's heights change significantly through their late teens or early twenties, their heads grow much more slowly after early childhood.

The length of a **baby's** head is one quarter of its total height.

Age 2 **Age 6** **Age 12**

The length of an **adult's** head is one seventh of its total height.

Applications

For Exercises 1–4, use the dot plot and histograms below. The graphs show the number of minutes it takes a class of students to travel to school.

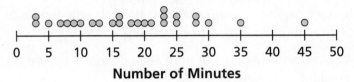

Student Travel Times

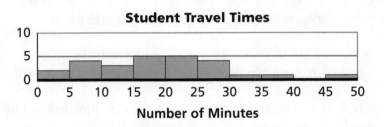

Student Travel Times

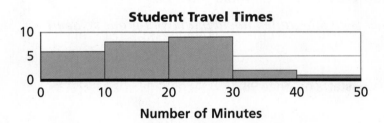

Student Travel Times

1. How many students spend exactly 10 minutes traveling to school?

2. Which histogram can you use to determine how many students spent at least 15 minutes traveling to school? Explain your reasoning.

3. How many students are in the class? Explain how you can use one of the histograms to find your answer.

4. What is the median time it takes the students to travel to school? Explain your reasoning.

For Exercises 5–9, use the graphs below. The graphs compare the percent of real juice found in different juice drinks.

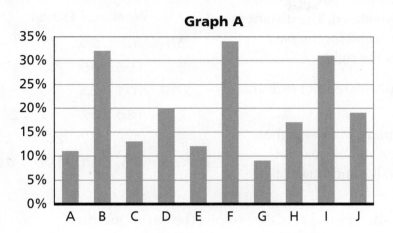

Graph A

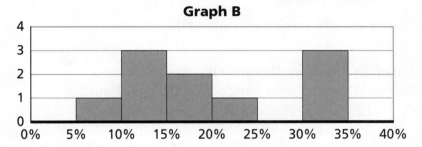

Graph B

5. **a.** Which juice drink(s) has the greatest percent of real juice? The least percent of real juice? Which graph did you use to find your answer? Explain why you chose that graph.

 b. For each juice you named in part (a), what percent of real juice does the drink contain? Which graph did you use? Explain.

6. **a.** Which graph can you use to find the percent of real juice found in a typical juice drink? Explain your reasoning.

 b. What is the typical percent of real juice? Explain your reasoning.

7. What title and axis labels would be appropriate for Graph A? For Graph B?

8. If you were given only Graph A, would you have enough information to draw Graph B? Explain your reasoning.

9. If you were given only Graph B, would you have enough information to draw Graph A? Explain your reasoning.

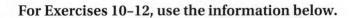
For Exercises 10–12, use the information below.

Jimena likes to hike in the hills. She drives to a new place almost every weekend. The distances Jimena traveled each weekend for the past 30 weekends are listed at the right.

Weekend Travel				
33	10	95	71	4
38	196	85	19	4
209	101	63	10	4
27	128	32	11	213
95	10	77	200	27
62	73	11	100	16

10. **a.** Draw a box-and-whisker plot to display the data.

   b. Why is the left-hand whisker of the box plot (between of the box plot the minimum value and Quartile 1) so short?

   c. Why is the right-hand whisker of the box plot (between Quartile 3 and the maximum value) so long?

   d. What information does the median give about the distances Jimena traveled?

   e. Find the mean of the distances. Compare the mean and the median distances. What does your comparison tell you about the distribution?

11. **a.** Draw a histogram showing the distribution of the data. Use an interval size of 20 miles.

   b. How many weekends did Jimena drive at least 20 miles but less than 40 miles? Explain how you can use the histogram to find your answer.

   c. How many weekends did Jimena drive 100 miles or more? Explain how you can use the histogram to find your answer.

   d. Use the median you found in Exercise 10. In what interval of the histogram does the median fall? How is this possible?

12. Consider the box plot you made in Exercise 10 and the histogram you made in Exercise 11.

   a. Compare the shape of the histogram to the shape of the box plot.

   b. How does the height of the first bar in the histogram relate to the length of the left-hand whisker in the box plot?

   c. How does the histogram help you understand the length of the right-hand whisker in the box plot?

For Exercises 13 and 14, use the jump-rope data from Problem 4.2.

13. Draw two box plots to compare one gender in Mrs. R's class to the same gender in Mr. K's class. For example, make box plots to compare either the girls from the two classes or the boys from the two classes. Did the girls (or boys) in one class do better than the girls (or boys) in the other class? Explain your reasoning.

14. Make a box plot for all the girls in Mrs. R's class and Mr. K's classes combined. Make a box plot for all the boys in Mrs. R's and Mr. K's classes combined. Compare the box plots. Who did better, the boys or the girls? Explain your reasoning.

15. **Multiple Choice** Which value is NOT needed to construct a box plot?

   A. upper quartile

   B. minimum value

   C. median

   D. mean

16. Tim and Kadisha used the box plots below.

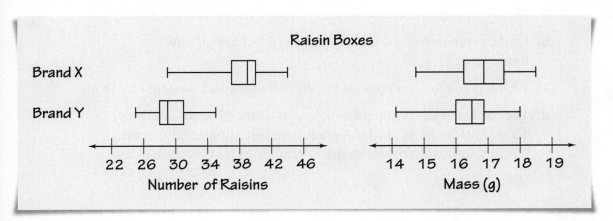

Raisin Boxes

Tim says that Brand X raisins are a better deal than Brand Y raisins because Brand X has more raisins in each box. Kadisha says that since each box has a mass of about 16 or 17 grams, the brands give you the same amount for your money. Do you agree with Tim or with Kadisha? Explain.

For Exercises 17–19, use the dot plots below. The dot plots show the weights of backpacks for students in Grades 1, 3, 5, and 7.

Grade 1 Backpack Weights

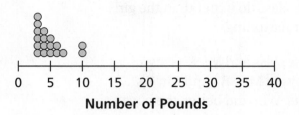

Number of Pounds

Grade 3 Backpack Weights

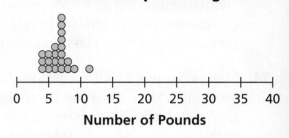

Number of Pounds

Grade 5 Backpack Weights

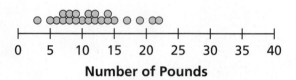

Number of Pounds

Grade 7 Backpack Weights

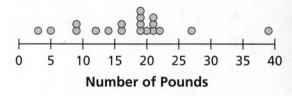

Number of Pounds

17. Use the dot plots above.

    a. Find the range of the data for each grade. Explain how you found it.

    b. Find the median of the data for each grade. Explain how you found it.

    c. Which grade has the greatest variation in backpack weights? Explain.

    d. The ranges of the backpack weights for Grades 1 and 3 are the same. The dot plots for these grades are very different, however. Identify some differences in the distributions for Grades 1 and 3

18. The box plots show the data from the dot plots on the previous page.

A.   **Backpack Weights**

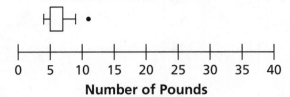

B.   **Backpack Weights**

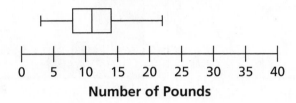

C.   **Backpack Weights**

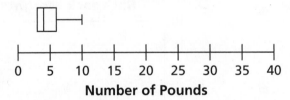

D.   **Backpack Weights**

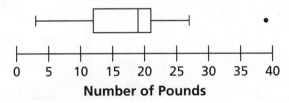

a. Which box plot shows the Grade 1 distribution? Explain.

b. Which box plot shows the Grade 3 distribution? Explain.

c. Which box plot shows the Grade 5 distribution? Explain.

d. Which box plot show the Grade 7 distribution? Explain.

e. Describe the shape of each distribution. Tell whether each is symmetric or skewed. Explain your reasoning.

19. The histograms below display the same data sets as the dot plots and box plots on the previous pages.

A.

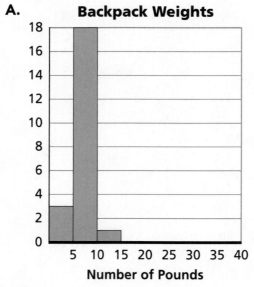

B.

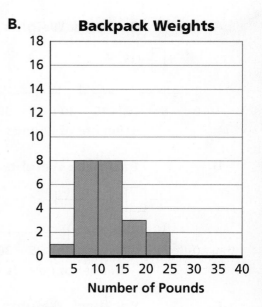

C.

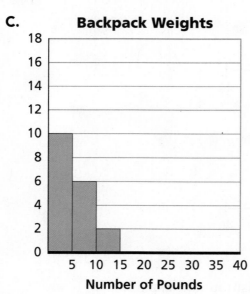

D.

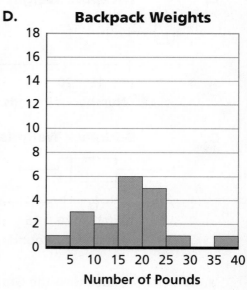

a. Which histogram shows the Grade 1 distribution? Explain.

b. Which histogram shows the Grade 3 distribution? Explain.

c. Which histogram shows the Grade 5 distribution? Explain.

d. Which histogram show the Grade 7 distribution? Explain.

e. Describe the shape of each distribution. Tell whether each is symmetric or skewed. Explain your reasoning.

For Exercises 20–23, use the box plots below. Each box plot shows the distribution of heights of 30 students at a particular grade level.

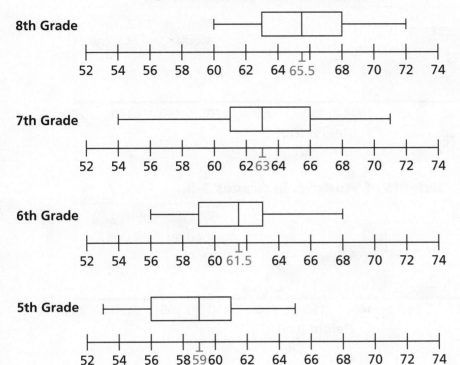

Heights of Middle-School Students

20. How much taller is an 8th grader than a 7th grader? Explain your reasoning.

21. On average, how much do students grow from Grade 5 to Grade 8? Explain.

22. Describe the shape of the Grade 6 distribution. Is it symmetric or skewed? Explain.

23. Describe the shape of the Grade 8 distribution. Is it symmetric or skewed? Explain.

For Exercises 24–26, use the histograms below. Each histogram shows the heights of 30 students in several grades.

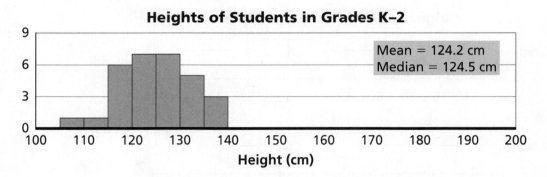

Heights of Students in Grades K–2

Mean = 124.2 cm
Median = 124.5 cm

Height (cm)

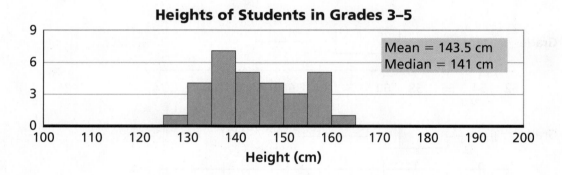

Heights of Students in Grades 3–5

Mean = 143.5 cm
Median = 141 cm

Height (cm)

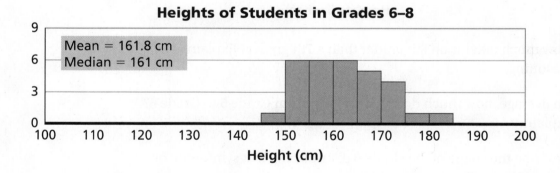

Heights of Students in Grades 6–8

Mean = 161.8 cm
Median = 161 cm

Height (cm)

24. On average, how much taller is a student in Grades 6–8 than a student in Grades K–2? Explain.

25. On average, how much taller is a student in Grades 6–8 than a student in Grades 3–5? Explain.

26. How is the shape of the histogram for Grades 3–5 different from the other histograms? Why might this be so?

Connections

27. Suppose the sum of the values in a data set is 250, and the mean is 25.

  a. Write a data set that fits this description.

  b. Do you think other students in your class wrote the same data set you did? Explain.

  c. What is the median of your data set? Does the median of a data set have to be close in value to the mean? Explain.

28. Each of the students in a seventh-grade class chose a number from 1 to 10 at random. The table below shows the results.

Number Chosen	Percent Who Chose the Number
1	1%
2	5%
3	12%
4	11%
5	10%
6	12%
7	30%
8	9%
9	7%
10	3%

  a. Draw a bar graph of the data.

  b. According to the data, is each number from 1 to 10 equally likely to be chosen?

  c. What is the mode of the data?

  d. Nine students chose the number 5. How many students are in Grade 7? Explain.

29. Moesha's mean score for six algebra quizzes is 79.5. She has misplaced a quiz. Her scores on the other quizzes are 82, 71, 83, 91, and 78. What is her missing score?

30. The tablet below shows data for the ages and heights of two 2012–2013 professional basketball teams.

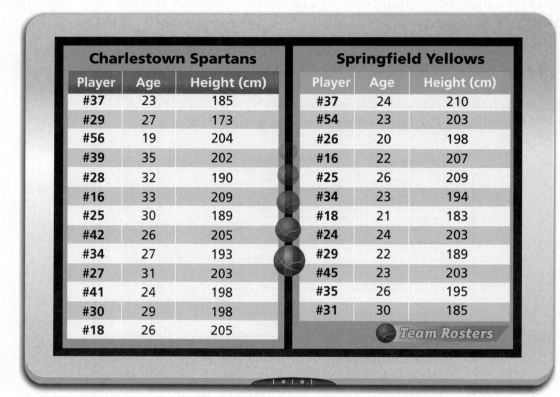

Charlestown Spartans			Springfield Yellows		
Player	Age	Height (cm)	Player	Age	Height (cm)
#37	23	185	#37	24	210
#29	27	173	#54	23	203
#56	19	204	#26	20	198
#39	35	202	#16	22	207
#28	32	190	#25	26	209
#16	33	209	#34	23	194
#25	30	189	#18	21	183
#42	26	205	#24	24	203
#34	27	193	#29	22	189
#27	31	203	#45	23	203
#41	24	198	#35	26	195
#30	29	198	#31	30	185
#18	26	205			

Team Rosters

a. Compare the ages of the two teams. Use statistics and graphs to support your answer.

b. Compare the heights of the two teams. Use statistics and graphs to support your answer.

c. Based on the data for these two teams, what age is a typical professional basketball player? What height is a typical professional basketball player? Do you think your generalizations are accurate? Why or why not?

Extensions

31. Alejandro and Katya are researching baseball facts. They find out that the durations of baseball games vary from game to game. The graph below shows the data Alejandro and Katya collected about the duration of baseball games.

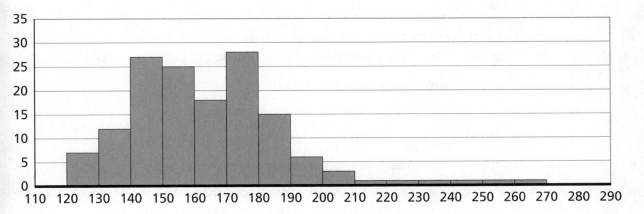

   a. What title and axis labels would be appropriate for this graph?

   b. Describe the shape of the graph. What does the shape tell you about the length of a typical baseball game?

   c. How many games are represented in the graph?

   d. Estimate the lower quartile, the median, and the upper quartile of the data distribution. What do these statistics tell you about the length of a typical baseball game?

32. Each box-and-whisker plot below has a median of 4. For each plot, provide a possible data set that would result in the distribution.

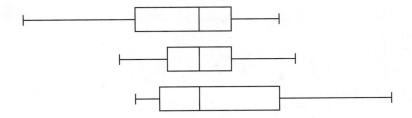

4

In this Investigation, you drew box plots and histograms to organize data into groups or intervals. You also used histograms and box plots to analyze and compare data distributions. The following questions will help you to summarize what you have learned.

Think about these questions. Discuss your ideas with other students and your teacher. Then write a summary of your findings in your notebook.

1. **Describe** how you can display data using a histogram.

2. **Describe** how you can display data using a box plot.

3. **a. How** can you use histograms to compare two data sets?

   b. How can you use box plots to compare two data sets?

4. Numerical data can be displayed using more than one type of graph. **How** do you decide when to use a dot plot, line plot, bar graph, histogram, or box plot?

Unit Project

Think about the survey you will be developing to gather information about middle school students.

 Which type of graph will best display the data you collect?

Common Core Mathematical Practices

As you worked on the Problems in this Investigation, you used prior knowledge to make sense of them. You also applied Mathematical Practices to solve the Problems. Think back over your work, the ways you thought about the Problems, and how you used Mathematical Practices.

Ken described his thoughts in the following way:

During Problem 4.3, and the rest of this Investigation, we realized that histograms and box plots group data. You don't see individual data values in those types of graphs. Histograms group data in intervals that you choose. Box plots group data into quartiles. Quartiles group the data into four equal parts.

It is easy to use graphs that show individual data values when the data values are not spread out and there aren't too many. When the values are spread out, or when there are a lot of data values, it's easier to use graphs that group data.

Common Core Standards for Mathematical Practice

MP4 Model with mathematics

 • What other Mathematical Practices can you identify in Ken's reasoning?

• Describe a Mathematical Practice that you and your classmates used to solve a different Problem in this Investigation.

Unit Project

Is Anyone Typical?

Use what you learned in this Unit to conduct a statistical investigation. Answer the question,

"What are some characteristics of a typical middle-school student?"

Complete your data collection, analysis, and interpretation. Then make a poster, write a report, or find another way to display your results. Your statistical investigation should consist of four parts.

Part 1: Asking Questions

Decide what information to gather. You should gather numerical data and categorical data. Your data may include physical characteristics, family characteristics, behaviors, and preferences or opinions.

Then, write clear and appropriate questions for your survey. Each person taking the survey should understand the questions. You may provide answer choices for some questions. For example, instead of asking, "What is your favorite movie?" you may ask, "Which of the following movies do you like the best?" and list several choices.

Part 2: Collecting Data

You can collect data from your class or from a larger group of students. Decide how to distribute and collect the survey.

Part 3: Analyzing the Data

Organize, display, and analyze your data. Think about the types of displays and the measures of center and variability that are most appropriate for each set of data.

Part 4: Interpreting the Results

Use the results of your analysis to describe some characteristics of the typical middle-school student. Is there a student that fits all the "typical" characteristics you found? Explain.

Looking Back

The Problems in this Unit helped you understand the process of statistical investigation. You learned how to:

• Distinguish between categorical data and numerical data

• Organize and represent data with tables, dot plots, line plots, frequency bar graphs, ordered-value bar graphs, histograms, and box-and-whisker plots

• Calculate and interpret measures of center and measures of spread

• Compare two or more distributions of data

Use Your Understanding: Data and Statistics

You can gather and analyze data in statistical investigations to help you make sense of the world around you. Follow these steps when you need to conduct an investigation.

• Pose questions.

• Collect data.

• Analyze data.

• Interpret the results.

For Exercises 1–4, use the information below.

Pet Ownership Survey Results

• Over 70 million households in the United States own a pet.
• About 6 out of 10 households in the United States own at least one pet.
• About two-fifths of pet owners have multiple pets.

1. What questions might have been asked in this survey?

2. Which questions from part (1) collected categorical data? Numerical data? Explain your reasoning.

3. What kinds of people may have responded to the survey?

4. Who might be interested in these results?

Explain Your Reasoning

5. Tyler decided to survey his classmates. He posed two questions:

What is your favorite kind of pet?
How many pets do you have?

Each classmate responded to the questions using student response systems. The answers appeared on the board.

Pet Survey							
2	3	3	17	cat	horse	cow	rabbit
5	9	5	0	dog	dog	cat	cat
6	2	6	1	cat	duck	rabbit	bird
1	5	14	6	cow	dog	dog	horse
8	3	2	2	bird	goat	fish	pig
1	2	3		dog	dog	rabbit	
0	4	21		horse	fish	dog	

a. Which data set goes with which question? Explain your reasoning.

b. Which data set includes categorical data?

c. Which data set includes numerical data?

d. Make a frequency table for each set of data.

6. Which types of graphs can be used to display categorical data? Explain your reasoning.

7. Which types of graphs can be used to display numerical data? Explain your reasoning.

For Exercises 8–11, use the information below.

A local candle-shop owner wonders which of his products lasts the longest. The owner does an experiment. He records the number of minutes that each candle burns. He completes 15 trials for each type of candle.

Candle-Burning Durations (minutes)

Trial	Brilliant Candle	Firelight Candle	Shimmering Candle
1	60	66	68
2	49	68	65
3	58	56	44
4	57	59	59
5	61	61	51
6	53	64	58
7	57	53	61
8	60	51	63
9	61	60	49
10	62	50	56
11	58	64	59
12	56	60	62
13	61	58	64
14	59	51	57
15	58	49	54

8. For each type of candle, find the median candle-burning time. Find the IQR. Explain how you found the median and IQR.

9. For each type of candle, find the mean candle-burning time. Find the MAD. Explain how you found the mean and MAD.

10. The dot plots, histograms, and box plots below show data on two of the candles. For each graph, identify the candle.

Dot Plot A

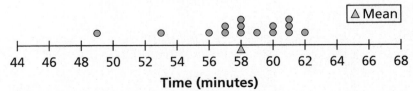

Time (minutes)

Dot Plot C

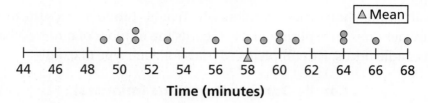

Time (minutes)

Histogram E

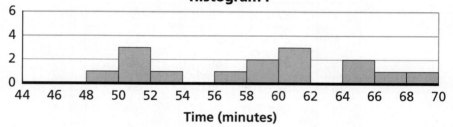

Time (minutes)

Histogram F

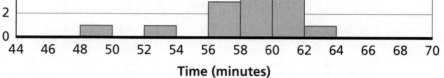

Time (minutes)

Box Plot G

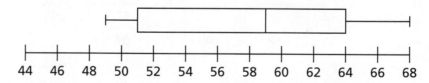

Box Plot H

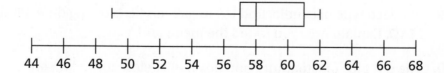

11. Use your answers for Exercises 8–10. Which candle burns for the longest amount of time? The shortest amount of time? Explain.

analyze Academic Vocabulary
To think about and understand facts and details about a given set of information. Analyzing can involve providing a written summary supported by factual information, a diagram, chart, table, or a combination of these.

related terms *examine, evaluate, determine, observe, investigate*

sample Analyze the following data to find the mean and the mode.

analizar Vocabulario académico
Pensar para comprender datos y detalles sobre un conjunto determinado de información dada. Analizar puede incluir un resumen escrito apoyado por información real, un diagrama, una gráfica, una tabla o una combinación de estos.

términos relacionados *examinar, evaluar, determinar, observar, investigar*

ejemplo Analiza los siguientes datos para hallar la media y la moda.

Getting to School

Student	Krista	Mike	Lupe	Kareem
Time (min)	10	15	20	10

Tiempo para ir a la escuela

Estudiante	Krista	Mike	Lupe	Kareem
Tiempo (minutos)	10	15	20	10

attribute An attribute is a characteristic or feature that is being investigated.

atributo Un atributo es una característica o cualidad que está siendo investigada.

box-and-whisker plot, or box plot A display that shows the distribution of values in a data set separated into four equal-size groups. A box plot is constructed from a five-number summary of the data.

gráfica de caja y bigotes o diagrama de caja Una representación que muestra la distribución de los valores de un conjunto de datos separados en cuatro grupos de igual tamaño. Un diagrama de caja se construye con un resumen de cinco números de los datos.

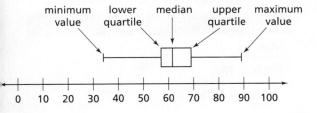

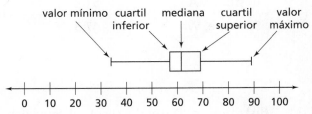

C **categorical data** Non-numerical data sets are categorical. For example, the responses to "What month were you born?" are categorical data. Frequency counts can be made of the values for a given category. The table below shows examples of categories and their possible values.

Category	Possible Values
Month people are born	January, February, March
Favorite color to wear	magenta, blue, yellow
Kinds of pets people have	cats, dogs, fish, horses

cluster A group of numerical data values that are close to one another.

For example, consider the data set 2, 2, 2, 2, 3, 3, 7, 7, 8, 9, 10, 11. There is a *cluster* of data values at 2 (or from 2 to 3) and a *gap* between data values 3 and 7.

D **data** Values such as counts, ratings, measurements, or opinions that are gathered to answer questions. The table below shows data for mean temperatures in three cities.

Daily Mean Temperatures

City	Mean Temperature (°F)
Mobile, AL	67.5
Boston, MA	51.3
Spokane, WA	47.3

distribution The entire set of collected data values, organized to show their frequency of occurrence. A distribution can be described using summary statistics and/or by referring to its shape.

datos categóricos Los conjuntos de datos no numéricos son categóricos. Por ejemplo, las respuestas a "¿En qué mes naciste?" son datos categóricos. Los conteos de frecuencia se pueden hacer a partir de los valores de una categoría dada. La siguiente tabla muestra ejemplos de categorías y sus posibles valores.

Categoría	Valores posibles
Mes de nacimiento de las personas	enero, febrero, marzo
Color preferido para vestir	magenta, azul, amarillo
Tipos de mascotas que tienen las personas	gatos, perros, peces, caballos

grupo Un grupo de valores de datos numéricos que están cercanos unos a otros

Por ejemplo, considera el conjunto de datos 2, 2, 2, 2, 3, 3, 7, 7, 8, 9, 10, 11. Hay un *grupo* de valores de datos en 2 (o de 2 a 3) y una *brecha* entre los valores de datos 3 y 7.

datos Valores como los conteos, las calificaciones, las mediciones o las opiniones que se recopilan para responder a las preguntas. Los datos de la siguiente tabla muestran las temperaturas medias en tres ciudades.

Temperaturas medias diarias

Ciudad	Temperatura media (°F)
Mobile, AL	67.5
Boston, MA	51.3
Spokane, WA	47.3

distribución Todo el conjunto de valores de datos recopilados, organizados para mostrar su frecuencia de incidencia. Una distribución se puede describir usando la estadística sumaria y/o haciendo referencia a su forma.

explain Academic Vocabulary
To give facts and details that make an idea easier to understand. Explaining can involve a written summary supported by a diagram, chart, table, or a combination of these.

related terms *analyze, clarify, describe, justify, tell*

sample Explain how to determine the mean and the mode of the data set 10, 15, 20, 10.

The mean is $\frac{10+15+20+10}{4} = 13.75$.

The mode of this data is 10 because 10 is the value that occurs most often.

explicar Vocabulario académico
Proporcionar datos y detalles que hagan que una idea sea más fácil de comprender. Explicar puede incluir un resumen escrito apoyado por un diagrama, una gráfica, una tabla o una combinación de estos.

términos relacionados *analizar, aclarar, describir, justificar, decir*

ejemplo Explica cómo determinar la media y la moda del conjunto de datos 10, 15, 20, 10.

La media es $\frac{10+15+20+10}{4} = 13.75$.

La moda de estos datos es 10 porque 10 es el valor que ocurre con mayor frecuencia.

frequency table A table that lists all data values, and uses tally marks or some other device to show the number of times each data value occurs.

tabla de frecuencias Una tabla que enumera todos los valores de datos y usa marcas de conteo o algún otro recurso para mostrar el número de veces que se produce cada valor de datos.

Lengths of Chinese Names
(From Name Lengths Table 1)

Number of Letters	Tally	Frequency
1		0
2		0
3		0
4		■
5	||	■
6	|||	■
7		■
8	||	■
9		■

G **gap** A value or several consecutive values, between the minimum and maximum observed data values, where no data value occurred.

For example, consider the data set 2, 2, 2, 2, 3, 3, 7, 7, 8, 9, 10, 11. There is a *cluster* of data values at 2 (or from 2 to 3) and a *gap* between data values 3 and 7.

brecha Un valor o varios valores consecutivos, entre los valores de datos mínimo y máximo observados, donde no se produjo ningún valor de datos.

Por ejemplo, considera el conjunto de datos 2, 2, 2, 2, 3, 3, 7, 7, 8, 9, 10, 11. Hay un *grupo* de valores de datos en 2 (o de 2 a 3) y una *brecha* entre los valores de datos 3 y 7.

....

H **histogram** A display that shows the distribution of numeric data. The range of data values, divided into intervals, is displayed on the horizontal axis. The vertical axis shows frequency in numbers or in percents. The height of the bar over each interval indicates the count or percent of data values in that interval.

The histogram below shows quality ratings for certain brands of peanut butter. The height of the bar over the interval from 20 to 30 is 4. This indicates that four brands of peanut butter have quality ratings greater than or equal to 20 and less than 30.

histograma Una representación que muestra la distribución de datos numéricos. El rango de valores de datos, dividido en intervalos, se representa en el eje horizontal. El eje vertical muestra la frecuencia en números o en porcentajes. La altura de la barra sobre cada intervalo indica el conteo o porcentaje de valores de datos en ese intervalo.

El siguiente histograma representa la calificación de la calidad de ciertas marcas de mantequilla de maní. La altura de la barra sobre el intervalo de 20 a 30 es 4. Esto indica que cuatro marcas de mantequilla de maní tienen una calificación mayor que o igual a 20 y menor que 30.

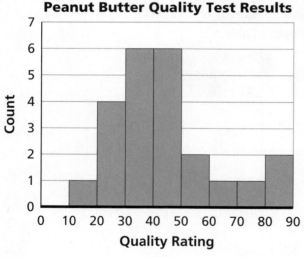

Peanut Butter Quality Test Results

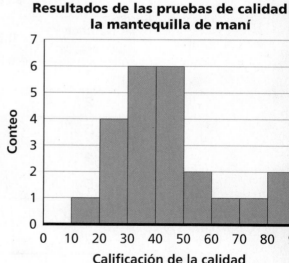

Resultados de las pruebas de calidad la mantequilla de maní

interquartile range (IQR) The difference of the values of the upper quartile (Q3) and the lower quartile (Q1).

In the box-and-whisker plot below, the upper quartile is 69, and the lower quartile is 58. The IQR is the difference 69–58, or 11.

$$IQR = 69 - 58 = 11$$

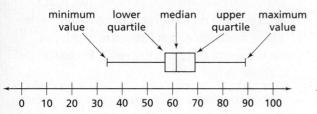

rango entre cuartiles (REC) La diferencia de los valores del cuartil superior (C3) y el cuartil inferior (C1).

En el siguiente diagrama de caja y bigotes, el cuartil superior es 69 y el cuartil inferior es 58. El REC es la diferencia de 69 a 58, u 11.

$$REC = 69 - 58 = 11$$

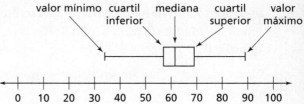

interval A continuous group of numbers. For example, a survey might collect data about people's ages. The responses could be grouped into intervals, such as 5–9, 9–12, and 12–16.

The interval 5–9 would include all ages 5 and older but not quite 9. If your ninth birthday were tomorrow, your data would fall into the interval 5–9.

intervalo Un grupo continuo de números. Por ejemplo, una encuesta puede recopilar datos sobre las edades de las personas. Las respuestas se pueden agrupar en intervalos, como 5 a 9, 9 a 12 y 12 a 16.

El intervalo de 5 a 9 incluiría todas las edades de 5 y mayores de cinco, pero no exactamente 9. Si tu noveno cumpleaños fuera mañana, tus datos se encontrarían en el intervalo de 5 a 9.

line plot A way to organize data along a number line where the ✗s (or other symbols) above a number represent how often each value is mentioned. A line plot made with dots is sometimes referred to as a dot plot.

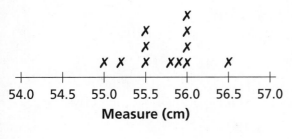

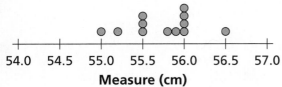

diagrama de puntos Una manera de organizar los datos a lo largo de una recta numérica donde las ✗ (u otros símbolos) colocadas encima de un número representan la frecuencia con que se menciona cada valor. Un diagrama de puntos hecho con puntos algunas veces se conoce como gráfica de puntos.

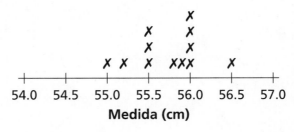

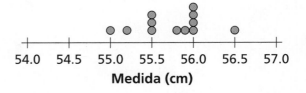

lower quartile The median of the data to the left of the median (assuming the data are listed from least value to greatest value).

For example, consider a data set with an odd number of items:

$$1, 2, 5, 6, 7, 8, 8, 10, 12, 15, 20$$

There are 11 items. The median of the data set is 8. (Six values are at or below 8 and six are at or above 8.) The median of the data to the left of the median (1, 2, 5, 6, 7) is 5. The lower quartile is 5.

Now consider a data set with an even number of items:

$$2, 3, 4, 5, 6, 6, 8, 8$$

There are eight items. The median of the data set is 5.5, the average of 5 and 6. The data items to the left of the median are 2, 3, 4, and 5. The median of these values is 3.5. The lower quartile is 3.5.

- -

M **maximum value** The data item with the greatest value in a data set. In the data set 2, 2, 2, 2, 3, 3, 7, 7, 8, 9, 10, 11, the maximum value is 11.

cuartil inferior La mediana de los datos a la izquierda de la mediana (asumiendo que los datos indicados van de menor a mayor).

Por ejemplo, considera un conjunto de un número impar de datos:

$$1, 2, 5, 6, 7, 8, 8, 10, 12, 15, 20$$

Hay 11 valores de datos. La mediana del conjunto de datos es 8. (Seis valores están en o encima de 8 y seis están en o debajo de 8). La mediana de los datos a la izquierda de la mediana (1, 2, 5, 6, 7) es 5. El cuartil inferior es 5.

Ahora considera un conjunto de un número par de datos:

$$2, 3, 4, 5, 6, 6, 8, 8$$

Hay ocho valores de datos. La mediana del conjunto de datos es 5.5, el promedio de 5 y 6. Los valores de datos a la izquierda de la mediana son 2, 3, 4 y 5. La mediana de estos valores es 3.5. El cuartil inferior es 3.5.

valor máximo El dato con el mayor valor en un conjunto de datos. En el conjunto de datos 2, 2, 2, 2, 3, 3, 7, 7, 8, 9, 10, 11, el valor máximo es 11.

mean The value found when all the data are combined and then redistributed evenly. For example, the total number of siblings for the data in the line plot below is 56. If all 19 students had the same number of siblings, they would each have about 3 siblings. Differences from the mean "balance out" so that the sum of differences below and above the mean equal 0. The mean of a set of data is the sum of the values divided by the number of values in the set.

Number of Siblings Students Have

```
              X
 X            X    X              X
 X       X    X    X    X    X
 X       X    X    X    X    X    X              X
 ─────────────────────────────────────────────────
 0   1   2    3    4    5    6    7    8
```
Number of Siblings

media El valor que se halla cuando todos los datos se combinan y luego se redistribuyen de manera uniforme. Por ejemplo, el número total de hermanos y hermanas en los datos del siguiente diagrama es 56. Si los 19 estudiantes tuvieran la misma cantidad de hermanos y hermanas, cada uno tendría aproximadamente 3 hermanos o hermanas. Las diferencias de la media se "equilibran" de manera que la suma de las diferencias por encima y por debajo de la media sea igual a 0. La media de un conjunto de datos es la suma de los valores dividida por el número de valores en el conjunto.

Número de hermanos y hermanas que tienen los estudiantes

```
              X
 X            X    X              X
 X       X    X    X    X    X
 X       X    X    X    X    X    X              X
 ─────────────────────────────────────────────────
 0   1   2    3    4    5    6    7    8
```
Número de hermanos y hermanas

mean absolute deviation (MAD) The average distance of all of the data values in a data set from the mean of the distribution.

desviación absoluta media (DAM) La distancia media de todos los valores de datos en un conjunto de datos a partir de la media de la distribución.

median The number that marks the midpoint of an ordered set of data. At least half of the values lie at or above the median, and at least half lie at or below the median. For the sibling data (0, 0, 0, 1, 1, 2, 2, 2, 2, 3, 3, 3, 4, 4, 5, 5, 5, 6, 8), the median of the distribution of siblings is 3 because the tenth (middle) value in the ordered set of 19 values is 3.

When a distribution contains an even number of data values, the median is computed by finding the average of the two middle data values in an ordered list of the data values. For example, the median of 1, 3, 7, 8, 25, and 30 is 7.5 because the data values 7 and 8 are third and fourth in the list of six data values.

mediana El número que marca el punto medio de un conjunto ordenado de datos. Por lo menos la mitad de los datos se encuentran en o encima de la mediana y por lo menos la mitad se encuentran en o debajo de la mediana. Para los datos de los hermanos y hermanas (0, 0, 0, 1, 1, 2, 2, 2, 2, 3, 3, 3, 4, 4, 5, 5, 5, 6, 8), la mediana de la distribución de hermanos y hermanas es 3 porque el décimo valor (el del medio) en el conjunto ordenado de 19 valores es 3.

Cuando una distribución contiene un número par de valores de datos, la mediana se calcula hallando el promedio de los dos valores de datos del medio en una lista ordenada de los valores de datos. Por ejemplo, la mediana de 1, 3, 7, 8, 25 y 30 es 7.5, porque los valores de datos 7 y 8 son tercero y cuarto en la lista de seis valores de datos.

minimum value The data item with the least value in a data set. In the data set 2, 2, 2, 2, 3, 3, 7, 7, 8, 9, 10, 11, the minimum value is 2.

valor mínimo El dato con el menor valor en un conjunto de datos. En el conjunto de datos 2, 2, 2, 2, 3, 3, 7, 7, 8, 9, 10, 11, el valor mínimo es 2.

....

mode The value that appears most frequently in a set of data. In the data set 2, 2, 2, 2, 3, 3, 7, 7, 8, 9, 10, 11, the mode is 2.

moda El valor que aparece con mayor frecuencia en un conjunto de datos. En el conjunto de datos 2, 2, 2, 2, 3, 3, 7, 7, 8, 9, 10, 11, la moda es 2.

....

N

numerical data Values that are numbers such as counts, measurements, and ratings. Here are some examples.

- Number of children in families
- Pulse rates (number of heart beats per minute)
- Heights
- Amounts of time people spend reading in one day
- Ratings such as: on a scale of 1 to 5 with 1 as "low interest," how would you rate your interest in participating in the school's field day?

datos numéricos Valores que son números como conteos, mediciones y calificaciones. Los siguientes son algunos ejemplos.

- Número de hijos e hijas en las familias
- Pulsaciones por minuto (número de latidos del corazón por minuto)
- Alturas
- Cantidades de tiempo que las personas pasan leyendo en un día
- Calificaciones como: en una escala de 1 a 5, en la que 1 representa "poco interés", ¿cómo calificarías tu interés por participar en el día de maniobras de tu escuela?

....

O

ordered-value bar graph A bar graph in which the bars are arranged by increasing (or decreasing) order of length.

gráfica de barras de valores ordenados Una gráfica de barras en la que las barras están ordenadas en orden de longitud creciente (o decreciente).

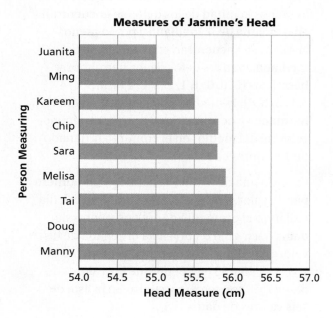

Measures of Jasmine's Head

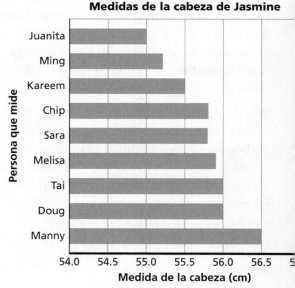

Medidas de la cabeza de Jasmine

outlier A value that lies far from the "center" of a distribution and is not like other values. *Outlier* is a relative term, but it indicates a data point that is much higher or much lower than the values that could be normally expected for the distribution.

To identify an outlier in a distribution represented by a boxplot, measure the distance between Q3 and any suspected outliers at the top of the range of data values; if this distance is more than $1.5 \times$ IQR, then the data value is an outlier. Likewise, if the distance between any data value at the low end of the range of values and Q1 is more than $1.5 \times$ IQR, then the data value is an outlier.

valor extremo Un valor que se encuentra lejos del "centro" de una distribución y no es como los demás valores. El *valor extremo* es un término relativo, pero indica un dato que es mucho más alto o mucho más bajo que los valores que se podrían esperar normalmente para la distribución.

Para identificar un valor extremo en una distribución representada por un diagrama de caja, se mide la distancia entre C3 y cualquier valor que se sospeche es extremo en la parte superior del rango de los valores de datos; si esta distancia es mayor que $1.5 \times$ REC, entonces el valor de datos es un valor extremo. Del mismo modo, si la distancia entre cualquier valor de datos en la parte inferior del rango de valores y C1 es mayor que $1.5 \times$ REC, entonces el valor de datos es un valor extremo.

predict Academic Vocabulary
To make an educated guess based on the analysis of real data.

related terms *estimate, survey, analyze, observe*

predecir Vocabulario académico
Hacer una suposición basada en el análisis de datos reales.

términos relacionados *estimar, encuestar, analizar, observar*

sample Dan knows that the mean life span of his type of tropical fish is 2 years. What other information could help Dan predict how long his fish will live?

ejemplo Dan sabe que la media de vida de su tipo de pez tropical es de 2 años. ¿Qué otra información podría ayudar a Dan a predecir cuánto vivirá su pez?

If Dan also knew the median life span he would have more information to predict how long his fish will live. The mean could be skewed because of one or more outliers.

Si Dan también supiera la mediana de vida, tendría más información para predecir cuánto vivirá su pez. La media podría estar sesgada debido a uno o más valores extremos.

quartile One of three points that divide a data set into four equal groups. The second quartile, Q2, is the median of the data set. The first quartile, Q1, is the median of the lower half of the data set. The third quartile, Q3, is the median of the upper half of the data set.

cuartil Uno de los tres puntos que dividen un conjunto de datos en cuatro grupos iguales. El segundo cuartil, C2, es la mediana del conjunto de datos. El primer cuartil, C1, es la mediana de la mitad inferior del conjunto de datos. El tercer cuartil, C3, es la mediana de la mitad superior del conjunto de datos.

R **range** The difference of the maximum value and the minimum value in a distribution. If you know the range of the data is 12 grams of sugar per serving, you know that the difference between the minimum and maximum values is 12 grams. For example, in the distribution 2, 2, 2, 2, 3, 3, 7, 7, 8, 9, 10, 11, the range of the data set is 9, because $11 - 2 = 9$.

rango La diferencia del valor máximo y el valor mínimo en una distribución. Si se sabe que el rango de los datos es 12 gramos de azúcar por porción, entonces se sabe que la diferencia entre el valor mínimo y el máximo es 12 gramos. Por ejemplo, en la distribución 2, 2, 2, 2, 3, 3, 7, 7, 8, 9, 10, 11, el rango del conjunto de datos es 9, porque $11 - 2 = 9$.

represent Academic Vocabulary
To stand for or take the place of something else. Symbols, equations, charts, and tables are often used to represent particular situations.

representar Vocabulario académico
Significar o tomar el lugar de algo más. Los símbolos, las ecuaciones, las gráficas y las tablas a menudo se usan para representar situaciones particulares.

related terms *symbolize, stand for*

términos relacionados *simbolizar, significar*

sample Jerry surveyed his classmates about the number of pets they have. He recorded his data in a table. Represent the results of Jerry's survey in a bar graph.

ejemplo Jerry hizo una encuesta entre sus compañeros de clase sobre el número de mascotas que tienen. Anotó sus datos en una tabla. Representa los resultados de la encuesta de Jerry en una gráfica de barras.

How Many Pets?

Number of Pets	Number of Students
0 pets	10
1 pet	11
2 or more pets	8

¿Cuántas mascotas?

Número de mascotas	Número de estudiantes
0 mascotas	10
1 mascota	11
2 o más mascotas	8

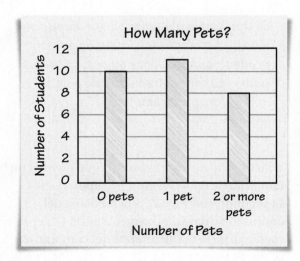

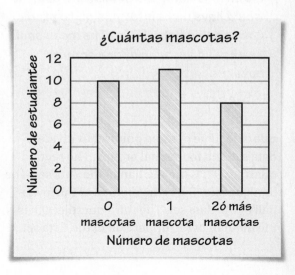

scale The size of the units on an axis of a graph or number line. For instance, each mark on the vertical axis might represent 10 units.

escala El tamaño de las unidades en un eje de una gráfica o recta numérica. Por ejemplo, cada marca en el eje vertical puede representar 10 unidades.

shape of a distribution The shape of a distribution can be described by identifying clusters and gaps, and by noting whether the distribution is symmetric or skewed.

forma de una distribución La forma de una distribución se puede describir al identificar grupos y brechas, y al observar si la distribución es simétrica o asimétrica.

skewed distribution Any distribution that is not symmetrical about the mean.

distribución asimétrica Cualquier distribución que no es simétrica alrededor de la media.

summary statistic A single number that conveys basic, but important, information about a distribution. Examples of summary statistics include the mean, median, mode, range, MAD, and IQR.

estadística sumaria Un solo número que transmite información básica, pero importante, sobre una distribución. Los ejemplos de la estadística sumaria incluyen la media, la mediana, la moda, el rango, la DAM y el REC.

symmetric distribution A distribution in which the mean and median are the same or almost the same, and in which the values above and below the mean form an approximate mirror image.

distribución simétrica Una distribución en la que la media y la mediana son iguales o casi iguales y en la que los valores por encima y por debajo de la media forman una imagen reflejada aproximada.

table A tool for organizing information in rows and columns. Tables let you list categories or values and then tally the occurrences.

tabla Una herramienta para organizar información en filas y columnas. Las tablas permiten que se hagan listas de categorías o de valores y luego se cuenten las incidencias.

Favorite Colors

Color	Number of Students
Red	6
White	15
Blue	9

Colores favoritos

Color	Número de estudiantes
Rojo	6
Blanco	15
Azul	9

U **upper quartile** The median of the data to the right of the median (assuming the data are listed from least value to greatest value).

For example, consider a data set with an odd number of items:

1, 2, 5, 6, 7, 8, 8, 10, 12, 15, 20

There are 11 items. The median of the data set is 8. (Six values are at or below 8 and six are at or above 8.) The median of the data to the right of the median (8, 10, 12, 15, and 20) is 12. The upper quartile is 12.

Now consider a data set with an even number of items:

2, 3, 4, 5, 6, 6, 8, 8

There are eight items. The median of the data set is 5.5, the average of 5 and 6. The data items to the right of the median are 6, 6, 8, and 8. The median of these values is 7, the average of 6 and 8. The upper quartile is 7.

cuartil superior La mediana de los datos a la derecha de la mediana (asumiendo que los datos indicados van de menor a mayor).

Por ejemplo, considera un conjunto de un número impar de datos:

1, 2, 5, 6, 7, 8, 8, 10, 12, 15, 20

Hay 11 valores de datos. La mediana del conjunto de datos es 8. (Seis valores están en o encima de 8 y seis están en o debajo de 8). La mediana de los datos a la derecha de la mediana (8, 10, 12, 15 y 20) es 12. El cuartil superior es 12.

Ahora considera un conjunto de un número par de datos:

2, 3, 4, 5, 6, 6, 8, 8

Hay ocho valores de datos. La mediana del conjunto de datos es 5.5, el promedio de 5 y 6. Los valores de datos a la derecha de la mediana son 6, 6, 8 y 8. La mediana de estos valores es 7, el promedio de 6 y 8. El cuartil superior es 7.

V **variability** An indication of how widely spread or closely clustered the data values are. Range, minimum and maximum values, and clusters in the distribution give some indication of variability. The variability of a distribution can also be measured by its IQR or MAD.

variabilidad Indicación de cuán dispersos o agrupados están los valores de datos. El rango, los valores mínimo y máximo, y los grupos en la distribución dan cierta indicación de variabilidad. La variabilidad de una distribución también se puede medir por su REC o por su DAM.

ndex

Index

Acknowledgments

Cover Design

Three Communication Design, Chicago

Text

113 American Pet Products Association

Data from *"2011–2012 National Pet Owners Survey"* from the American Pet Products Association (APPA).

Photographs

Photo locators denoted as follows: Top (T), Center (C), Bottom (B), Left (L), Right (R), Background (Bkgd)

002 Solent News/Splash News/Newscom; **003** WaterFrame/Alamy; **013** (CL) Plusphoto/AmanaimagesRF/Getty Images, (CR) iStockPhoto/Thinkstock, (BC) Jeayesy/Fotolia, **022** Lculig/Shutterstock; **047** Solent News/Splash News/Newscom.